W9-BVC-395

PIECE BY PIECE

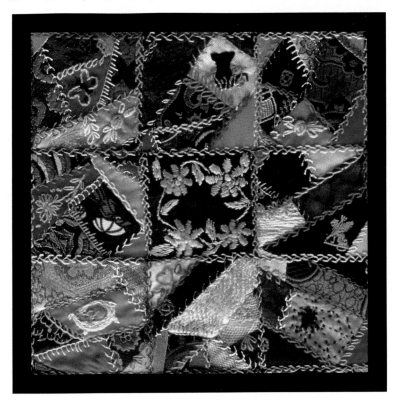

PIECE BY PIECE

THE COMPLETE BOOK OF QUILTMAKING

DIANNE FINNEGAN

PRINCIPAL PHOTOGRAPHY BY
GEORDIE McCRAE

PRENTICE
HALL
PRESS

NEW YORK LONDON TORONTO SYDNEY TOKYO SINGAPORE

Prentice Hall Press
15 Columbus Circle
New York, New York 10023

First published in Australasia in 1990 by
Simon & Schuster Australia
7 Grosvenor Place, Brookvale NSW 2100

Prentice Hall Press and
colophons are registered
trademarks of Simon & Schuster, Inc.

A Paramount Communications Company
Sydney   New York   London   Toronto   Tokyo   Singapore

Library of Congress
Catalog Card Number 90-70747
ISBN: 0-13-675869-X

Designed by Deborah Brash/Brash Designs
Diagrams drawn by Anna Warren
Typeset in Hong Kong by Setrite
Produced by Mandarin Offset
Printed and bound in Hong Kong

First Prentice Hall Press Edition

ACKNOWLEDGEMENTS

My thanks go to the quiltmakers throughout Australia
who appear in this book, and to my photographer
Geordie McCrae and my editor Susan Morris-Yates.
I would also like to thank Paddy Child Green and her
husband Irvine for organising the photography in
Melbourne. Finally, my family — Terry, Donald,
Thomas and Patrick.

METRIC CONVERSION

Generally there has been a standard "rounding out" of measurements in this book.

While 2.5 cm has been regarded to be equal to 1 in., métric measurements have been given to the nearest centimetre equivalent of imperial measurements. However, in the case of very small measurements, the metric figure has been rounded out to the nearest half centimetre. Thus, 5 mm is given to represent ¼ in.

For ease in construction, other measurements have been rounded out to the nearest appropriate divisible numbers, particularly for drafting.

COPYRIGHT IN THE QUILTS

The copyright in the individual photographic images of the various quilts reproduced in this book rests with the maker of each quilt. The quiltmakers' names appear in the captions beside each image. Any enquiries, particularly about further reproduction, should be directed to the quiltmaker.

DIAGRAM KEY

— · — · —
Cutting line

· · · · · · · · · · · · · · · · ·
Fold line

— — — —
Sewing line

▬▬▬▬▬▬
Design line

————————
Construction line

CONTENTS

Quilt on piano: *The Garden Beyond* by Susan McIver. 233 cm x 161 cm (91 ½ in. x 63 ½ in.). Machine pieced in Attic Window design. Hand quilted. Cushions by Diane Dowe

INTRODUCTION

THESE days it is hard to know where quiltmaking stops being a traditional craft and where it evolves into new and exciting art forms. The traditional (and primary) function of quilts was as bedcovers — and many are still made for that purpose today. But now quilted works can be made, amongst other things, into clothing and innovative pieces of pure art for the wall.

Whatever the intention of the quiltmaker, quilts are an opportunity to design on a large scale, to play with colour and fabrics in ways that are sometimes even more flexible than those of the traditional arts. With each new quilt comes the opportunity to work out relationships between shapes and colours, to resolve problems and improve on past efforts. Whether you work within the traditions or stretch the form to its limits, quiltmaking is one of the most absorbing of pastimes.

In *Piece By Piece* all the different components that make up this fascinating subject have been drawn together. From the beginning (the basic requirements and things you need to know) to the end (finishing and caring for your quilts) this book can be used at various levels, depending on the needs of the reader.

All the quilts in this book are Australian and often give traditional patterns a fresh look. The quilts have been chosen not only because they are well designed, but because they exemplify a variety of quiltmaking techniques approached innovatively. Quite often you will notice cross references in the text because so many of the quilts demonstrate different

Jocelyn Campbell at work in her studio.

elements of design and technique and could be used as examples for many different aspects of quiltmaking. Following up these references is not essential, but you will learn from comparing the different treatments quiltmakers give to the same feature. It will help you to develop your eye and to learn to analyse the elements of the quilt and why some quilts work so well. These lessons can then be applied to your own work.

The evolving tradition of quiltmaking in Australia is briefly considered, providing a context for contemporary quilts. Then there are two major sections. The first explores elements of colour and design to help provide an understanding of the design process and to help discover how certain colour effects can be achieved. In addition to the "rules" are many descriptions and illustrations of contemporary Australian quilts, as well as interviews with selected quiltmakers who discuss their approach to their work. Here theory can be seen being put into practice — in exciting ways. And, of course, there is the very practical section on quilt construction covering piecing, appliqué and quilting. Again this section can be used at different levels. Some, for example, may need basic instructions for sewing, while others may wish to draft blocks of their own choice. Still others may be inspired by the diversity of quilts illustrated and wish to design an original pattern. With a practical knowledge of drafting it is possible to draw up blocks of any size, freeing you from the need to rely on templates published in books and magazines. With a sound knowledge of technique you will not be frustrated by inaccuracy or limited in what you can attempt.

I hope the combination of text, diagrams and photographs will encourage and inspire you. Enjoy!

DIANNE FINNEGAN
Sydney, 1990

QUILTMAKING IN AUSTRALIA

In 1927 a writer for Coats Clark of Glasgow, manufacturers of thread, proclaimed the virtues of quilting in an article entitled "Quilting and its Newest Developments" which appeared in *The Needlewoman*. "Once more," he wrote, "a cycle of fashion has been completed, and quilting, which had a vogue in our great-grandmothers' day for the making of cosy coverlets and petticoats, again invades the realms of dress, but this time makes its appeal through its decorative qualities rather than for its power of giving warmth."

Quilts have certainly always been made for their warmth, although these days their decorative appeal often outweighs this utilitarian aspect. They usually comprise three layers: the top, a layer of batting for warmth and loft (thickness), and a lining or backing. The three layers are held together by lines of stitching known as quilting, and the pattern made by this stitching can be an important element in the overall design. The top may be a whole cloth, on which the quilting becomes the focus of the design, or may be patchwork. The patchwork can be either a pieced top, made from many patches sewn together, or can be created from shapes appliquéd onto a background fabric. Such quilts, not unnaturally, are known as appliqué quilts.

Quilts have been a source of industrious needlework throughout the last two hundred years of Australian history, although not produced in the same profusion as American quilts, where they were essential

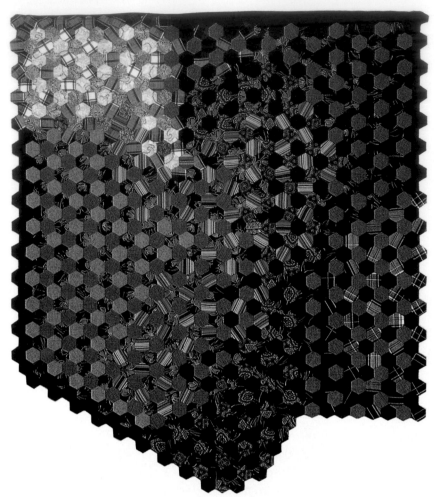

Search for School Grey by Nancy Tingey. 145 cm x 125 cm (57 in. x 49 in.). Hand stitched hexagons in English Paper Method. Tied

bedcoverings. Even before white men settled in the country, possum skins were patched together by the Aborigines to make warm coverings.

Over the two hundred years since white settlement there has been a succession of styles which have enjoyed periods of popularity. In her historical overview *Patchwork Quilts in Australia*, Margaret Rolfe gives the results of her research into old Australian quilts. Many of the styles of quilts that Margaret describes are still being made today, either in the traditional manner, or extended in new directions by contemporary quiltmakers. To paraphrase the Coats Clark writer, "everything old is new again". Even without

conscious copying, there are certain styles that have come back into fashion. An overview of the progression of styles in Australian quiltmaking heralds the range and diversity seen today. The following descriptions are based on Margaret Rolfe's research:

The prison reformer Elizabeth Fry arranged for the convict women being transported to the fledgling colony in New South Wales to be provided with the equipment to make quilts on the voyage from England. In this manner they could learn to sew at the same time as producing something that could be sold to earn them money in the colony.

Hexagon quilts were an early favourite, and even today are frequently used, particularly as an

Dullflower No. 4: The Everlasting by Marjorie Coleman. 170 cm x 166 cm (67 in. x 65½ in.). Hand sprayed, hand and machine pieced and appliquéd. Hand quilted

introduction for those who have no experience in quiltmaking. Among contemporary quilters Nancy Tingey's hexagon quilts have gone beyond the rosettes of old to use the shape as a medium for her art, while Alison Muir creates a three-dimensional effect in her *Executive Ladder* (see page 112), which is based on the Baby Blocks variation of the hexagon.

Medallion quilts, with a central feature surrounded by decorative borders, are still popular. Trudy Brodie's *Miniature Medallion Quilt* (see page 82) displays the simplicity of some of the early medallion quilts, while Wendy Holland's *Pale Ladies* (see page 146) is a less constrained version of the style.

Broderie Perse, the technique by which motifs from one fabric are appliquéd onto another background, evolved from the time when chintz was very expensive. Motifs from a prized chintz background were transferred to a less expensive material. Helen Macartney's miniature *Flora* (see page 14) piles one motif onto another, using this style.

Appliqué quilts have continued to be popular, and quiltmakers in different parts of Australia use the

Flora by Helen Macartney. 41 cm x 41 cm (16 in. x 16 in.). Broderie Perse appliqué by machine. Hand quilted

technique to produce strikingly different results. In Western Australia, Marjorie Coleman uses appliqué to portray the flora and fauna that she lives amongst (see page 13). And in Queensland Denise Vanderlugt uses brilliant colours to record butterflies, flowers and other tropical scenes.

Made of many scraps of fabric ranging from silks to velvets, and secured to the backing fabric with embroidery stitches, Crazy Patch quilts were popular in Victorian times. Marjorie Coleman's *Townhouse* (see page 16) is no less restrained than those earlier quilts.

Embroidery stitches continue to be used for embellishment in a few modern quilts. Prue Socha used couched thread and French knots in *Japanese Hillside* (see page 17), while Kerry Gavin used backstitching to emphasise the flowers in her wholecloth quilt,

Heirloom of Wildflowers (see page 136). Wholecloth quilts are traditionally solid cream or white and provide a large fabric area on which to show off the quilting design.

During periods of economic restraint even the smallest scraps of fabric were assembled into a quilt to provide warmth. Lois Densham's *Healing Blanket* (see page 18) recalls the old "waggas", bedcoverings often made of chaff

Red Berries of the Rainforest by Denise Vanderlugt. 200 cm x 200 cm (78½ in. x 78½ in.). Hand appliquéd with embroidered details. Hand quilted

bags or woollen suit material samples. Often there were no regular surface patterns as shape depended on the available fabric. Appearance was secondary to function. They might be stuffed with old blankets or woollen clothing — anything for warmth.

To raise funds during the World War I, signature quilts were made: people donated money to record their signature on the quilt. The Quilters' Guild Signature Quilt (see page 152), made to raise money for the Guild's bicentennial exhibition, continues this tradition.

When even the smallest strip was utilised, Log Cabin quilts were a sensible design choice. Popular in America, the Log Cabin is composed of hundreds of narrow strips of fabric sewn around squares. Half the block is light and half dark, and both Pamela Tawton (see page 19) and Greg Somerville (see page 25) have played with the tones to develop original designs.

Pieced quilts are made up of shapes cut out in several fabrics and sewn together to create a design. They are the most popular form of quiltmaking in Australia today, as they have been in America for many years. The

Townhouse by Marjorie Coleman. 128 cm x 106 cm (50½ in. x 41½ in.). Hand appliquéd and machine pieced. Hand quilted

Japanese Hillside by Prue Socha. 260 cm x 246 cm (102½ in. x 97 in.). Machine pieced. Hand quilted, chain stitched leaves

most popular arrangement for a quilt is in blocks. Easy to handle because each block can be sewn separately before they are all joined together, the thousands of patterns provide ample opportunity to learn the craft while exploring the possibilities of combinations of fabrics.

Not all pieced quilts are based on blocks; for instance when a

large number of strips of fabric have accumulated from other projects a strippie quilt might be made. This could be randomly stripped or carefully planned. My *Terra Australis* (see page 34) had to be made in a hurry to replace a quilt that had been burnt. I had been sent a disparate range of fabrics from women throughout Australia who had heard of the

fire. They ranged from silks to furnishing fabrics. I needed to sew them in a way that was quick, showed off the fabrics and said something about the country. Strip piecing reminded me of rock strata, probably because of my background in geomorphology.

Strips can also be specially cut for a project, and seminole quilts using such strips of fabric were

Healing Blanket by Lois Densham. 185 cm x 150 cm (73 in. x 59 in.). Crazy patchwork in wool blanket samples built on cotton voile, outlined heavily with hand and machine blanket stitch developed by the Seminole Indians in response to the introduction of the sewing machine. Ann Moten's seminole quilt (see page 86) is a contemporary version of this technique. Because the strips are rearranged and joined again, they can develop into block patterns and thus appear complex. This method can be used to create blocks for repeat block quilts. Many quilts have units that can be sewn in this way so that individual pieces are never cut.

Instead of building a quilt from units of blocks or strips, some prefer to work with the entire quilt top, perhaps creating pieced pictures. In *Pools of Peace* Christa Roksandic used curved seams to create a scene (see page 83). Trudy Billingsley with her straight seams used the whole quilt top to develop her theme. Although the works are broken into units for ease of sewing, these divisions are not apparent in the whole quilt.

Quiltmaking in Australia has a distinctive flavour. The country's remoteness has isolated it from the mainstream of quiltmaking in the United States and in Britain. Although basic techniques have been imported from these countries, the absence of a strong local tradition of quiltmaking has resulted in an unfettered

Moonriver by Pamela Tawton. 255 cm x 195 cm (100½ in. x 77 in.). Machine pieced. Hand quilted. Off-centre Log Cabin

approach to the art. The colours and designs that have emerged here have an air of freshness and ingenuity.

The quilts illustrated in this book have been chosen to represent simple traditional

patterns, contemporary interpretations of old designs, and bold new directions. They provide an overview of the diversity of contemporary work.

Japanese Family Crest Quilt by Diane Dowe. 300 cm x 200 cm (118 ins. x 78½ in.). Hand stencilled and quilted. *The Not Too Available Kimono* by Marjorie Patterson. Machine pieced. Hand quilted

DESIGN
AND
COLOUR

Quilts are the product of the creativity of their maker: their sense of colour and design, and their craftsmanship. The visual impact depends on the relationship of colour and design, and on good needlework, too.

Many find that quiltmaking, a medium in which they can test out relationships between colours and patterns, is a non-threatening introduction to artistic creation. Quilting techniques are mostly straightforward and the materials required are usually readily available without needing to make a major investment in equipment. Quiltmaking provides an opportunity for self-expression within a structured framework in which the level of difficulty can be controlled. For beginners, reproducing old patterns, while trying to match fabrics as closely as possible, reduces the need to make decisions while perfecting technique. With growing technical competence comes a need to express oneself, either by varying an old design or developing original work. The quilt provides a large canvas for this creative self-expression.

In an attempt to work out how effects are achieved and why they are successful, quilters are frequently led to study colour and design. Rather than set out the principles in a formal manner, let's look at the following quilts and see how they work.

INSPIRATION

Many people come to quiltmaking through their appreciation of old quilts. Unlike many arts and crafts, a first quilt can be very effective, and several of the quilts in this book are first efforts. Choices may be reduced while learning. Follow a simple, old pattern and try matching fabrics to the quilt you have appreciated, then you can concentrate on putting it together. Trudy Billingsley's *Maple Leaf* (see page 27), a very simple nine-patch in only two colours, makes a strong graphic statement. The choice of pattern and fabrics made, the top was sewn, repeating an ordered sequence. It was then quilted to the batting and lining. The repetitive nature

of the work is simple and effective.

Megan Terry's *Milky Way* is a vibrant, modern interpretation of a traditional block, Ohio Star. Once again the pattern is simple, but in this case complexity is introduced by the use of many prints. The choice of fabrics stamps Megan's personality on a traditional pattern. Each block presents a new opportunity for decisions about the placement of fabric.

These two block repeat quilts demonstrate that the fabric placement for the whole quilt can be planned before sewing and the blocks replicated, or the blocks can be planned individually, then the arrangement decided towards the end.

Dianne Firth is a landscape architect whose geometric bent is reflected in her choice of structured grids. She frequently

Nine Patch by Dianne Firth. 122 cm x 122 cm (48 in. x 48 in.). Machine pieced. Hand quilted

uses a repeat block, although it may not be a traditional design, and often incorporates a glowing centre representing a light source, creating it with a gradation from darker to lighter tones towards the middle of the quilt. Dianne sees the quilt whole at an early stage in the design process, and does not have to agonise over the placement of fabrics. Her *Nine Patch* illustrates these preoccu-

pations. A very simple block set on the point gains interest from the gradation of colour.

For some the quilt evolves slowly, with a lot of consideration and planning. Prue Socha designs from scratch, not relying on traditional patterns. She cuts and lays out her fabrics in a possible order and considers them for days, changing them around, adding and subtracting until she

finds the overall effect pleasing. Her quilts appear structurally simple, belying the considered arrangement that goes into their design (see page 17).

With her first massive hexagon quilt (not illustrated), Nancy Tingey used a traditional technique to sew the hexagons, but her arrangement is original, and her edges, particularly, a departure. She had some

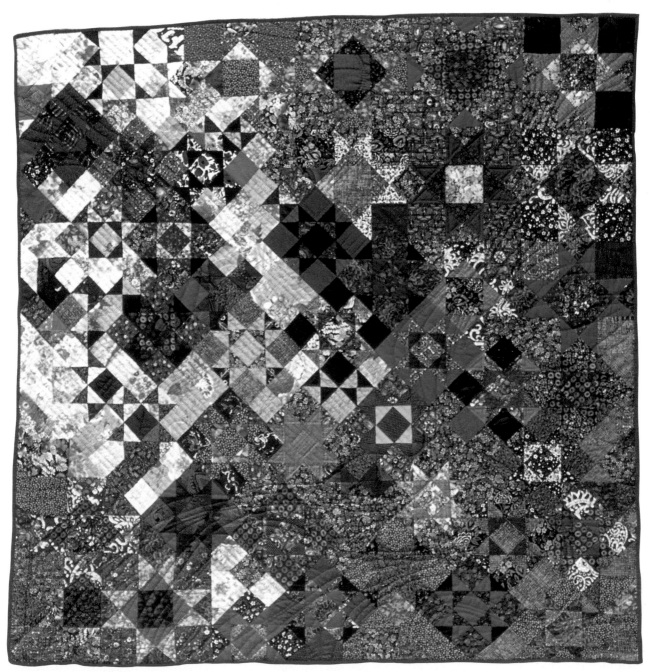

Milky Way by Megan Terry. 128 cm x 126 cm (50½ in. x 49½ in.). Hand pieced. Hand quilted. Nine-patch Ohio Star block in two sizes

logistical problems: "It just grew, and I used to have to carry the whole quilt around with me because each new piece related to all the other pieces that were already there, and I did not work in groups. In some ways it was the most exciting quilt I've ever made because it was unplanned and yet it had an internal structure that was based on relationships in my family . . . When the last child had started school I began to lay things out completely before I started stitching. Otherwise I wasted time unpicking."

Less controlled, chance combinations are explored by quilt artists like Wendy Holland and Greg Somerville. Wendy may start with large blocks of fabric joined in a random manner. Slashed and rejoined in several directions the work gains complexity, and new relationships between fabrics, tones and shapes emerge. Insertions add to the whole, and help to unify all the elements. Her idiosyncratic choice of unexpected fabrics and their juxtaposition adds a spark to her work and sets it apart.

Greg produces quite a different result in *Implicate Order No. 4*. Starting with strips, he joins, slashes and recombines, often using a quick machine technique known as seminole. However, the strips he uses are not a regular width, and the cuts are also not a consistent width, so the regularity of normal seminole is lost and the technique is not obvious. Such an apparently unstructured approach needs a sure eye to unify the whole. Nevertheless, it is a good exercise for someone wanting to break away from using the traditional block.

For many quiltmakers the Australian landscape and environment is a source of inspiration. Both Prue Socha and

Implicate Order No. 4 by Greg Somerville. 187 cm x 174 cm (73 ½ in. x 68 ½ in.). Painted and found fabrics. Machine appliquéd and pieced. Machine quilted.

Trudy Billingsley are keen observers, and holidays provide an opportunity to absorb the environment, particularly its colours. These impressions are then translated into fabric with very different results.

By overhearing the chance remark of a tourist that Australian wildflowers are dull, Marjorie Coleman was prompted to create a whole series of quilts based upon the so-called "dullflowers" (see page 13). Nancy Tingey, however, became fascinated with the foliage on a castle wall during a trip to England. The relationship between that organic form and the wall supporting it led her to make quilts that grew outwards from the centre. She lost interest in the rectilinear format of most quilts and transferred her attention to the leaves and background wall. The uneven

edge is shown up against the wall on which the quilt is hung. Compare the quilt *Hanging Garden* with a wall that Nancy photographed, and the relationship between inspiration and finished product can be seen.

Naturally the imagination of individual quiltmakers is a great source of inspiration. Greg Somerville and Lois Densham (see page 18) explore their thoughts and emotions in making their quilts. Greg's *Implicate Order* series explores a scientific concept about different kinds of order. A book on Islamic art inspired the underlying pattern for *Implicate Order No. 2*. It starts out as a patchwork piece then, towards the edge, the background is incorporated into the design as some of the pieces are dropped out. The quilting pattern maintains the regular piecing right across the quilt so that even

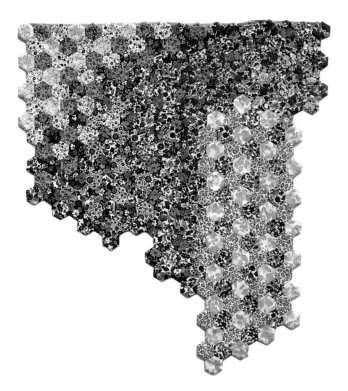

Above: Photograph by Nancy Tingey of ivy on a wall

Left: *Hanging Garden* by Nancy Tingey. 91 cm x 81 cm
(36 in. x 32 in.). Hand stitched hexagons by English Paper
Method. Tied

Implicate Order No. 2 by Greg Somerville. 250 cm x 190 cm (98½ in. x 75 in.). Hand appliquéd and pieced. Hand quilted.

though the order in the piecing appears to have broken down, the pattern is maintained by the quilting line.

Lois Densham's *Healing Blanket* (see page 18), made from Onkaparinga blanket samples, a dressing gown and army uniforms, developed from a realisation that those particular colours cheered her when she was feeling low. The red creates a sense of warmth and the back is a calm green landscape.

Other crafts also provide inspiration. Ann Lhuede's *Celtic Keys* (see page 105) owes much of its origins to the *Book of Kells*, but the colourful interpretation is very much her own. Diane Dowe stencilled family crests on her dramatic *Japanese Family Crest Quilt* (see page 20).

DESIGN

Most quilts are pieced: they are composed of small pieces of fabric sewn together in a regular, repeating pattern. The simplest way to divide up the surface is with a single, tessellated shape. Squares, rectangles, triangles and hexagons are the most common. Helen Macartney's *Banksia*, composed of squares, could not be easier to piece. Her *Bush Garden* (see page 126) is also a one-patch, in this case a triangle. The impact comes from the same design silk screened in several colour ways. Compare this to Fiona Gavens's *The Hollow Tree*. Both have very few templates or shapes, but Fiona has created a semi-abstract work whose colour placement and shading evoke a familiar image.

The majority of quilts appear

Banksia by Helen Macartney. 75 cm x 55 cm (29½ in. x 21½ in.). Hand screen-printed. Machine pieced. Hand quilted

unified and harmonious because they consist of repeating pieced blocks. If the blocks are large, as in Trudy Billingsley's *Maple Leaf*, the design appears bold. By using only two colours, red and white, she creates positive and negative areas, and the eye moves from the patterns in one colour to the other.

If the shapes are very small and many fabrics are used, then a rich visual texture is created. An occasional touch of a bright accent colour introduces a focal point for the eye to rest on. The red centre of a Log Cabin design fulfils this function.

The blocks are commonly divided up into regular grids

and the individual shapes that make up blocks are often squares and triangles. There are thousands of such patterns, some varied only by differences in the placement of light, medium and dark coloured fabrics. Most patterns are symmetrical, falling about one or two axes that divide the block in half along the midpoint of opposite sides, or diagonally from corner to corner. The setting, or positioning, of the blocks can make even identical blocks read quite differently.

Although pieced quilts are the ones that are most commonly developed on repeat blocks, some appliqué quilts also fall into this category. Jeanette Parsons's *1000*

Maple Leaf by Trudy Billingsley.
190 cm x 140 cm (75 in. x 55 in.).
Machine pieced. Hand quilted

The Hollow Tree by Fiona Gavens. 140 cm x 60 cm (55 in. x 23½ in.). Machine pieced and quilted

Hours is an example (see page 94). More usually, though, appliqué quilts have designs that cover the whole quilt top. Elva Hine's *Floral Heirloom* is one (see page 94), based on a medallion design. Like a pieced medallion it has a central feature, surrounded by borders. The outside border is pieced, containing the naturalistic shapes of the flowers.

Blocks and borders can be dispensed with entirely: Marjorie Coleman often uses the whole surface of the quilt to express her ideas in her appliqué quilts. Because it is easier to introduce curved lines in appliqué, most pictorial quilts use this technique. However, quiltmakers like Trudy Billingsley draw up landscapes and subdivide the design into irregular blocks to facilitate piecing. For both methods, the design is drawn up full-scale so that pattern pieces or templates can be made.

I have already mentioned the less formal approach taken by Wendy Holland in some of her quilts. Balance is not achieved by symmetry, but by placement of

Skyscraping by Christa Roksandic. 148 cm x 122 cm (58½ in. x 48 in.). Machine pieced. Hand quilted

colour, placement of lights and darks, and shape. This would seem to be a quick way to obtain a result because there are no templates, but for the whole to work the same principles of balance, repetition, contrast, dominance, rhythm and unity apply.

Drafting quilts that fall into these categories will be covered in the section on Quilt Construction. Any quilt can be drafted and sewn using a few basic techniques — as you will see!

COLOUR

Most quiltmakers have no training in colour and design; they develop a colour sense from putting fabrics together in quilts, observing what works and what fails. But some have come to quiltmaking with a background in the arts, drawn by the tactile pleasure of handling the fabric. Nancy Tingey, who trained as an artist and is experienced in stained-glass work, explains the attraction. "I'm really a painter but this was another way of playing around with colour. Working with stained glass is similar to quilting because you are selecting from something that is already there, in this case the fabric rather than a piece of glass. I find it a marvellous way of using colour because mixing colour in painting can limit you because you can be afraid of trying new combinations. With fabric you can try a piece and then discard it if it doesn't work. In watercolour painting you have to know what you are doing when you put the paint down. Quilts allow you to become more adventurous because you can combine colours

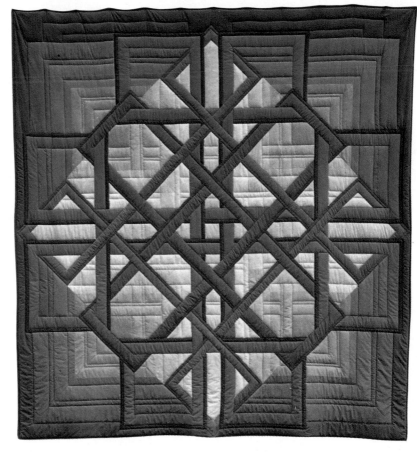

Eternal Knot by Fiona Gavens. 280 cm x 270 cm (110 in. x 106½ in.). Hand dyed. Machine pieced and quilted

and patterns that you would not normally dare to try and you can find that, yes, that is exciting, that really works."

Most quilts are based on traditional block designs, and having chosen the pattern, the next decision is the location of tones within the block. These variations in tone or value are achieved by the arrangement of light, medium and dark fabrics, an arrangement that is usually consistent from one block to the next. If the gradation from light to medium to dark falls in even steps, then the arrangement will seem to be a natural progression.

This progression is best illustrated by looking at a *grey scale* (Diagram 1), which has an even gradation of greys ranging in tones from white to black. The

number of steps in the scale can vary, but it is difficult for the eye to register more than seven. Christa Roksandic's *Skyscraping* uses many shades of grey to suggest perspective and three-dimensional buildings. Fiona Gavens used colour gradations in her early Eternal Knot series of quilts, but she had to dye her own fabrics to obtain an even gradation of values.

Different values of a colour can be produced by adding white or black, to give tints and shades. If two colours are close in value it is sometimes hard to tell which

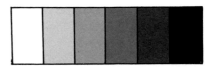

I Six-step grey scale

Floriade (detail) by Judy Turner. 275 cm x 259 cm (108½ in. x 102 in.). Strip quilted by machine. Hand finished

colour is lighter. View them through your eyelashes. This cuts the colour and makes it easier to position them on a grey scale. Alternatively, photostat your fabrics. This eliminates colour completely, giving only the tones of the fabric.

Some designs use the placement of values to give a three-dimensional effect. Susan McIver's Attic Window quilt *The Garden Beyond* (see page 8) has the grey and black windowsills consistently placed to give the impression of looking through a window. Alison Muir's *Executive Ladder* (see page 112) is an original interpretation of Baby Blocks that acquires depth by systematically shading the facets of each block.

The way you see a value is influenced by the fabrics that surround it. Both Adèle Outteridge and Judy Turner make use of the reversal technique in their quilts respectively called *Monkey Wrench* (see page 56) and *Floriade*. In both the lattice remains constant while the blocks and strips change in value. When the lattice is darker or lighter than

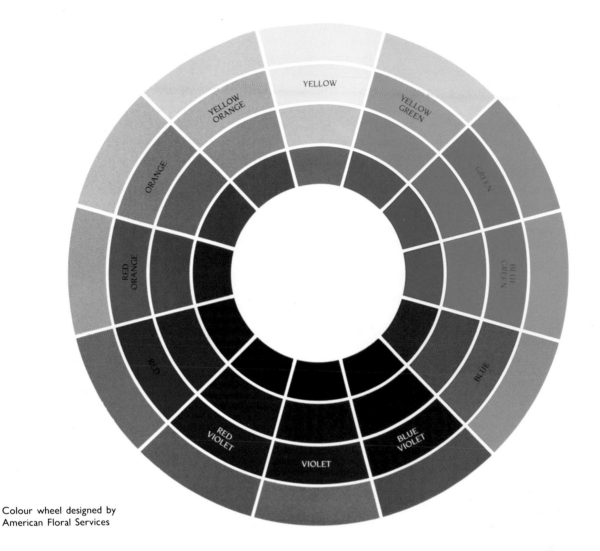

Colour wheel designed by
American Floral Services

the surrounding fabric, it stands out; when it is close in value, it tends to merge and become less intrusive.

Judy graded the strips from dark at the bottom to light towards the top of the quilt. This tone sequence feels comfortable because we are naturally used to the weight or darkness of the earth below and the lightness of the sky above.

The three values can be close together on the grey scale so the differences are subtle, or they can be far apart, giving a much bolder effect. Black against white is the greatest possible contrast, and the black and white pieces Marjorie Coleman has used in *Townhouse* make it dynamic (see page 16).

Conversely, Adèle Outteridge has used solids close in value in her *Miniature Star* (see page 90) so that the interest lies in the colour, not the tone.

Combinations of printed fabric can produce unexpected effects. A print may provide a touch of a complementary colour or introduce a colour that may be repeated in another fabric. If adjacent prints contain the same colour or tone, it may carry across the seamline, blurring the edges of the piece.

The next consideration after tone or value is colour placement. The first quilts a beginner makes are often in safe colours that match the existing decor of a room. The enjoyment found in

putting fabrics together can lead to more adventurous combinations in later quilts.

Although random effects can be exciting, the colouring of a quilt benefits from careful planning. A scrap quilt put together with no consideration of the relationship of colours from one patch to the next is less likely to please the eye. Colour theory should help to organise a colour scheme for a quilt.

No one should approach a quilt purely from a set of rules on colour, but they can be useful guides. The starting point for any discussion about colour is the *colour wheel* (Diagram 2). The main colours of the spectrum are set out in a circle in the order in which they naturally merge into one another.

The three *primary colours* from which all other colours can be mixed are red, yellow and blue. Between them are the *secondary colours* orange, green and purple. The *tertiary colours* are mixed from adjacent primary and secondary colours. Thus the colour wheel runs red, red-purple, purple, purple-blue, blue, blue-green, green, green-yellow, yellow, yellow-orange, orange, orange-red. Each colour on the colour wheel in its pure state is sometimes referred to as a *hue*. Barbara Macey's *Mind Series — Stream of Consciousness* uses the progression on the colour wheel to suggest the dynamic, optimistic evolution of thought.

Certain combinations of colours are known to work. The *neutrals*, brown and grey, are safe, as is a *monochromatic arrangement*, where only one colour is used in combination with its tints and shades — a technique used by Mae Bolton in *Boston Commons*. The use of two, three, or even more, adjacent colours on the colour wheel creates a peaceful, pleasing effect. This is known as an *analogous harmony*, something that Suzanne Hamilton uses in

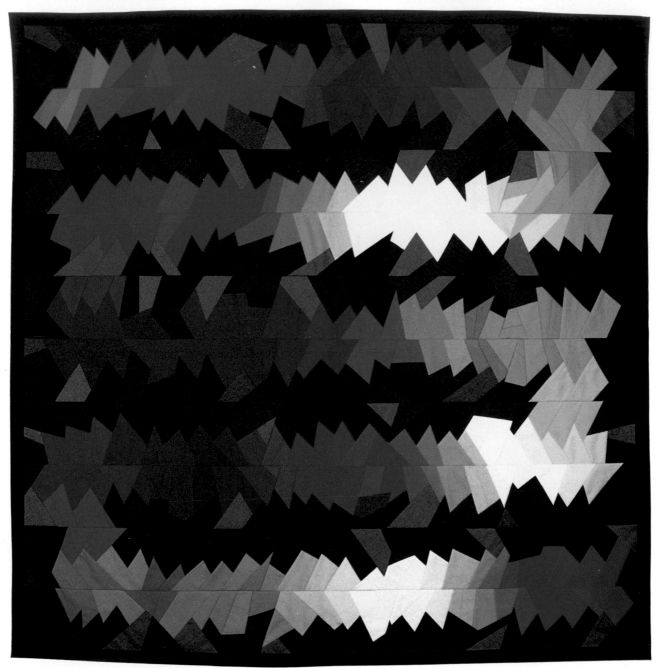

Mind Series — Stream of Consciousness by Barbara Macey, 150 cm x 150 cm (59 in. x 59 in.). Machine pieced and quilted

her curved seam miniature, *Amish Path*. If a colour is too dominant its effect can be reduced by placing it next to one of its adjacent colours.

Colours opposite each other on the colour wheel are harmonious, and are known as *complementary colours*. In their saturated form they intensify each other, and when their chroma is reduced by adding a complementary colour or grey, they harmonise well. A *split complementary* is another harmonious combination; it is achieved when one of the complementaries is replaced by the colours on either side of it on the colour wheel. If three colours equally spaced on the wheel are used, they form a *triadic harmony*. In *Terra Australis* (see page 34) I limited myself to a triadic harmony of the secondary colours.

The use of a *contrast* colour, one far from another on the colour

wheel, may add impact to a quilt. As happens with value, the same colour reads differently according to the surrounding colour. This is known as *simultaneous contrast* and actually extends the range of fabrics because the same piece seems to vary in brightness according to the surrounding fabrics.

If these rules about colour are followed too slavishly, your quilt might lack spark. Anyway, if you use prints it is unlikely that the colours in all the prints will conform to the rules. Nevertheless the "rules" are handy as a guide.

Besides the guide rules above there are a few other points to remember; for example, certain colours can be very strong and may need to be used sparingly: red, yellow and orange tend to advance, or jump out at you. Also remember that many fabrics have an off-white background, and if

another fabric that incorporates a true white is used it will be painfully obvious. It may be worth test dyeing the fabric with true white in cold tea to turn the white to ecru. However, the tea may also dull some of the other colours unacceptably, in which case it is easier not to use the fabric in the quilt.

Sometimes a dash of an accent, a touch of brightness, can liven up a quilt. Margot Child sometimes incorporates a print with some yellow in it to add a spark (see page 43), while Elizabeth Ashley used hot pink in her *Pink Sampler* (see page 58). A small quantity of a complement in a similar value can liven up a quilt, for instance a touch of orange beside blue, or red against green.

A much more subtle effect is *transparency*, which is obtained by finding the midpoint between two colours so that neither colour

Above: *Amish Path* by Suzanne Hamilton. 52 cm x 42 cm (20½ in. x 16½ in.). Hand pieced and quilted.

Left: *Boston Commons* by Mae Bolton. 259 cm x 188 cm (102 in. x 74 in.). Hand pieced and quilted

Terra Australis by Dianne Finnegan. 230 cm x 160 cm (90½ in. x 63 in.). Machine strip pieced and quilted

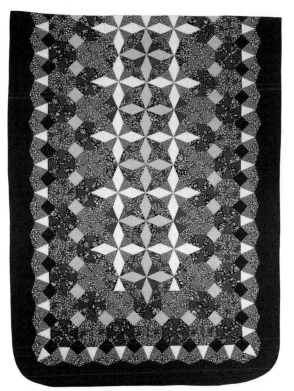

Above: *Kaleidoscope* by Valerie Gordon. 258 cm x 190 cm (101 ½ in. x 75 in.). Machine pieced. Hand quilted. Based on Eight-Point Star

Left: *Carousel* by Susan McIver. 208 cm x 132 cm (82 in. x 52 in.). Machine pieced. Hand quilted. Kaleidoscope design based on Eight-Point Star

appears to have the dominant weight. The new colour must be exactly the right value. By placing this intermediary colour between the others, there is a sense of overlap, of seeing through one colour to the other beneath. Barbara Macey achieves this effect with her run of colours (see page 32).

To understand how important colour is in quilts, compare two based on the same design. Both Susan McIver and Valerie Gordon have used a Kaleidoscope pattern, but they look like very different designs. Susan's *Carousel* is the more traditional, and has been designed to sweep the eye around the piecing in circles, even though it is all pieced in straight lines. The effect is enhanced by the quilting. Valerie Gordon's quilt, *Kaleidoscope*, however, is

more static, but more complex. By changing the placement of values around the edge, she has created a border and the circles are less obvious.

Because it is unlikely that you will find precisely the right colours to suit a colouration based on colour theory, these principles are only a guide. As soon as you move from solids to prints it is likely that more colours will be introduced than you had planned. Perhaps you can exploit these chance combinations. When in doubt, or if you are uncertain about how a particular effect is achieved, the theory is there to be consulted.

FABRIC

The first view of a quilt is usually from a distance, and the initial impact is made by the design and colour. On close inspection the individual pieces of fabric and their light-reflective qualities create interest, and the quilting pattern is more obvious. Thus, after deciding on design and colour, the next choice is fabric. Although this sequence of decisions is a logical approach to creating traditional quilts, the fabrics themselves may suggest design directions, and the steps in the decision making can be circuitous.

A quilt derives its *tactile texture* from the surface quality of the fabrics and from the quilting line,

Stripes of Callais by Dianne Neumann. 238 cm x 204 cm (93½ in. x 80½ in.). Hand pieced and quilted. Sampler

Black and White by Helen Gritscher. 240 cm x 180 cm (94½ in. x 71 in.). Machine pieced. Hand quilted

which can be machined in a hard line, finely handquilted in a softer line, or emphasised with thick thread and long stitches. In most quilts dress weight fabrics are used. These are practical as bedcovers, they can be machine washed, but there is little variation in surface texture.

More adventurous quilts such as wall hangings, which need not be washed, are not limited by such practical constraints. Like the Victorian Crazy Patch quilts that once graced grand pianos, they can be made from anything ranging from velvet to silk. This allows different weaves and sheens to be introduced, giving the quilt texture to the touch.

Another means of introducing the impression of texture into a quilt is by varying the size of the print in the fabric design. This *visual texture* is achieved by placing one simulated texture against another, as in *Black and*

White by Helen Gritscher. Solids act as flat planes of colour, an effect that Dianne Firth uses in her explorations of light in *Nine Patch* (see page 22). When used in combination with prints, the expanses of colour can seem very strong, and may need to be broken up with quilting lines.

Prints vary in design, combinations of colours and in scale. By mixing them a work can acquire a richness and complexity transcending the piecing pattern. Compare Mae Bolton's *Boston Commons* (see page 33), with its monochromatic colour scheme, close values and similar prints, with Judy Turner's assorted print size and colours in *Floriade* (see page 30). The first has a serene effect that invites appreciation of the fine handwork and a concentration on the quilting, while the second provides an exciting explosion of vibrant colour and visual texture.

The feature in the print can be used to carry through a theme by centring the pieces on a particular feature such as a flower or a bird, or the features can be chopped haphazardly, their impact caused by the chance juxtapositions with other fabrics.

If stripes are to be used uniformly great care must be taken to match them accurately, as Dianne Neumann has done in her intricately pieced *Stripes of Calais*, while Wendy Holland uses stripes exclusively in *Japanese Stripes* (see page 38). Helen Macartney's *Tartanella* uses plaids, lending sophistication to a simple design. If cut off the straight line, stripes and checks can add a naive quality to a work. Wendy Holland uses checks cut off the grain for impact.

To decide whether the combination of fabrics will suit the quilt you plan, pile them up, stand back and consider them.

Tartanella by Helen Macartney. 208 cm x 166 cm (82 in. x 65½ in.). Machine pieced. Hand quilted

Japanese Stripes by Wendy Holland. 156 cm x 132 cm (61 ½ in. x 52 in.). Machine pieced. Hand quilted

Broulee by Marli Popple. 152 cm x 120 cm (60 in. x 47 in.). Hand dyed with indigo and fibre reactive dyes. Machine strip pieced and quilted

Squint to eliminate some of the colour and to see if any element jumps out at you unexpectedly. If possible, follow Prue Socha's advice and leave the fabrics lying around for several days, varying them as your ideas change. If the effect is too bland, consider adding a small accent — perhaps a dark fabric would help. Consider varying the scale of the prints. Some very small granny prints might look boring together, but with some medium-sized and larger prints they may take on new life. When very large prints are cut up, individual pieces become like completely different fabrics because parts of the fabric design are isolated.

If the solids you have chosen

are too strong, you can substitute a small monotone print which will read as a solid but have a slightly more visual texture, in keeping with the rest of the range. Remember that a solid light fabric used as a background will intensify the other colours in the quilt. You can see this in Elva Hine's red and green appliqué in *Floral Heirloom* (see page 94) which shows up strongly against the solid cream background. The Amish on the other hand used black to highlight their strong, simple designs which were pieced in solids. As quilting shows up far better on solids than on prints, the Amish were, in this way, able to showcase their fine handquilting.

The range of colours

commercially available is not sufficient for some. Trudy Billingsley chooses to overdye some of her fabrics so that they are close in colour, and if Wendy Holland does not like a fabric, she might silkscreen-print over it, changing its character completely. Fiona Gavens was able to achieve careful gradations in colour by dyeing her own fabric in her earlier Eternal Knot quilts (see page 29), and Jan Irvine uses the fabric as a blank canvas upon which she stencils and airbrushes her designs, for example in *Ellipse* II.

Instead of relying on printed fabrics, Diane Dowe created her own fabric designs. Starting with white fabric, she stencilled Japanese family crests and created a ripple border for her dramatic black and white Japanese quilt (see page 20). Unable to achieve the results she wanted with commercial fabrics, Marli Popple uses a variety of dyeing techniques to broaden the range of effects in her quilts. The cotton in *Broulee* is hand dyed with fibre reactive and indigo dyes. The fabrics were dyed, cut into strips, and rearranged many

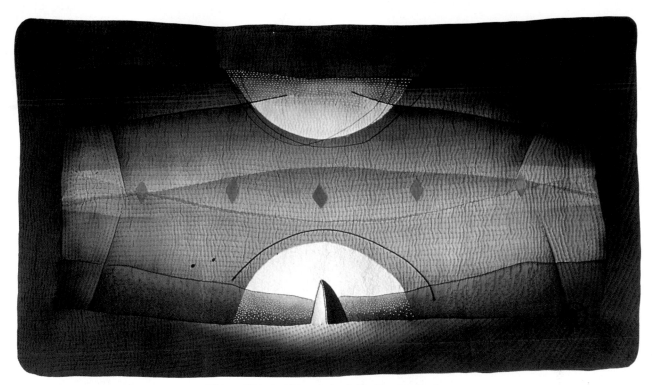

Ellipse II by Jan Irvine. 120 cm x 180 cm (47 in. x 71 in.). Airbrush dyed silk. Hand quilted

times to achieve the feel and effects Marli wanted. The waves are composed of indigo dyed fabric that was tied and dyed, while the sky is procion dyed, then the cloud effect achieved by bleaching certain areas. The red ribbon birds are made with a Japanese knot to represent a wish or a prayer. Helen Macartney's *Banksia* (see page 26) is a very straightforward square design, given subtlety by the use of silkscreened fabrics in different colourways in which the design is replicated in several sets of colours.

A complete account of fabric dyeing and painting is beyond the scope of this book, but Proctor and Lewis's *Surface Design for Fabric* (1984) provides a good treatment of the field.

QUILTING

Quilting is the embellishment on patchwork that distinguishes it from other forms of sewing. The quilting stitch not only fulfils the function of holding the top, batting and lining together, but presents an opportunity to unify the foreground derived from the piecing or appliqué, which provide the positive elements of the design, with the negative space of the background fabric. It gives a three-dimensional, sculptured effect to the work.

The quilting design can echo the patchwork, complement it with a unifying design or introduce an entirely different pattern that forms a visual tension by the contrast. A wholecloth quilt, with no patchwork as a distraction, provides the expanse of the quilt top to develop a design.

Patchwork can be analysed in terms of positive and negative space. In general the pieced or appliquéd design reads as the positive space or foreground, and the background fabric acts as negative space. If the background fabric has fewer quilting lines to hold it down than the design, it will pop up and, by default, become an important area in the overall design. This can be a disconcerting effect. By considering spaces on the quilt as either positive or negative, and planning the quilting accordingly, the problem can be resolved. A sampler quilt provides a fresh opportunity to resolve this in each block. Susan McIver's *Carly's Quilt* (see page 65) allowed her the opportunity to make different design decisions for each block. You can see from the picture how she has treated the background areas and the sashes.

On a pieced quilt, the quilting can be done in the ditch, that is,

Bush Window by Barbara Ward. 210 cm x 150 cm (82½ in. x 59 in.). Hand appliquéd, embroidered and quilted along the seam line, which reinforces the lines of the piecing design. Christa Roksandic uses this effect to emphasise the shapes in *Pools of Peace* (see page 83). A design can also be emphasised by outline quilting, that is, quilting 5 mm ($\frac{1}{4}$ in.) out from the seam line. A series of quilting lines that echo the design to create a concentric ripple effect is called, naturally enough, echo quilting. It is an effect usually combined with Hawaiian Appliqué.

Another approach is to superimpose an entirely different design on the pieced block. Curved quilting lines always look good on geometric piecing because of the contrast between the hard and soft edges.

Many old traditional quilts use filler patterns, such as rows of parallel lines, to quilt down the background, thus puffing up and isolating the central features (see diagram on page 127). Cross hatching is a popular filler pattern, with the amount of space between the lines depending on the piecing or appliqué. The lines are quilted diagonally because they show up better on the bias of the fabric. Avoid spacing the quilting lines so that they run into the crossing points of seamlines. A repeat shape like a clamshell can look attractive and has the benefit of repeatedly using but a single shape to draft the pattern onto the fabric.

Appliqué is shown to advantage if it is ditch quilted because it puffs up the shapes, and another line of outline quilting will further flatten the background. The curved shapes of appliqué look good in a field of cross hatching and old quilts often used this combination. Jeanette Parsons's *1000 Hours* uses a straight line grid on the diagonal as a filler pattern (see page 94). The

blocks are set on the point and, instead of sashing, they are separated by a lattice of quilting. A quilting pattern fills the triangles left around the edge of the blocks when they are set in a border.

Practical considerations can determine the quilting design. For instance, seam allowances are more difficult to quilt through, which often results in the need to use a less attractive longer stitch. So, if possible, the quilting pattern should avoid them. Thus, hexagons pieced by the English Paper Method are traditionally outline quilted, 5 mm ($\frac{1}{4}$ in.) from the seam line, avoiding the extra thickness of the seams.

Large areas intentionally left to display quilting can be provided by alternate plain blocks and by sashes and borders. The extreme is the wholecloth quilt, where the interest is entirely concentrated on the quilting.

The wholecloth quilt often consists of a central feature isolated by cross hatching and surrounded by at least one quilted border which may also incorporate some cross hatching. Rosettes, wreaths, mandalas, scrolls, feathers, cables, fans, shells and other stylised organic forms often feature in such designs. Traditionally the quilting is symmetrical, with patterns forming mirror images. One or more of these quilting patterns can be used in quilts with alternating plain blocks, in sashing or in borders. The success of the design is enhanced by the well-turned corner of a border, so the border pattern must be carefully constructed to mitre or turn in some attractive manner, otherwise the movement of your eye will not flow around the bend.

Barbara Ward's *Bush Window* contains the appliqué within a

thin fabric border which is then surrounded in turn by a quilted border on the background fabric. The quilted flora continues the appliquéd shapes.

Many contemporary quilters overlook repetitive patterns in quilting in favour of an overall pattern that may relate to the patchwork or contrast with it. You can see that in this manner the quilting extends the story in Jocelyn Campbell's *Turtles at the Waterhole* (see page 92), and on my *Terra Australis* (see page 34), bands of stripped fabrics are united by quilting representing weathering patterns on rocks. In *Ellipse II* (see page 39) Jan Irvine dispenses with patchwork altogether and uses the fabric as a canvas for her painted picture. The quilting stitches are large and lines of quilting are closely spaced to give a textured effect.

QUILTMAKERS

The diversity of quilt designs in Australia reflects the differences in approach taken by individual quiltmakers. Their attitudes, design sources, fabric collections, methods of construction and place of work all vary enormously. To give an idea of the variety here is a series of accounts by some quiltmakers about themselves and their work.

Margot Child has a sound background in needlework, and enjoys interpreting simple, traditional patterns. For her the challenge lies in putting together a multitude of fabrics in scrap quilts. She works by hand and does not rush any of the stages. Her quilts are usually for family, so she is not pressured by commercial deadlines.

Marjorie Coleman is a Western

Australian quiltmaker whose driving urge is to create wall quilts that express her thoughts and surroundings. The technique is secondary to the result, although to be unobtrusive it must be good.

Like Marjorie, Trudy Billingsley was introduced to quilts when she lived overseas for a time. In childhood she was guided by her parents to observe the world around her closely and this early training has resulted in her landscape quilts and pieced pictures.

A background in fine arts, a love of textiles and exposure to fine old quilts in England prompted Wendy Holland to try making some herself. She soon abandoned complex patterns to explore chance combinations of diverse fabrics, many of them old.

Margaret Rolfe, from Canberra, wanted to design block patterns that were typically Australian rather than relying on traditional patterns. Using a computer has aided this design process. A number of successful books are the result.

Adèle Outteridge made many traditional quilts before her interest in fabric manipulation led her to experiment with painted fabrics in new ways. Chance developments led her in many directions.

Diane Dowe is an artist whose interest in patchwork is expressed in many media; she discusses a montage of her work, the influences, materials she uses, and some of the results.

MARGOT CHILD

When I was young it was an accepted part of family life to use "spare" time productively, so we knitted, embroidered and mended

Margot Child hand quilting a single Irish Chain in a hoop

while listening to the wireless at night. For me this has carried over to the age of television and I rarely watch it without a quilt on my lap — to be idle is vaguely sinful. My mother was a fine embroiderer and passed on her interest in good hand sewing to me. After leaving school I planned a career in science and determinedly did not learn to type or put together a "glory box" in passive resistance to the prevailing expectations for girls. However, like many of my friends at university, I knitted and sewed my own clothes.

Beautiful old quilts seen on a visit to America inspired me to make my own. Although my first quilts were appliqué designs, I was quickly converted to pieced quilts after seeing some of Wendy Holland's early work in an exhibition. Wendy's quilts appeal to me strongly, and I found her workshops revelatory. I joined a group at the Embroiderers' Guild where Elizabeth Burton was teaching and began to learn about colour and techniques. I don't myself aspire to make "art" and

recognise my limitations, but I keep my eyes open to new experiences. In most of my work I stick to simple, universal designs, usually squares and triangles, and explore the myriad possibilities of rearrangement. I rarely look beyond patterns like Pinwheels, Attic Window or simple stars. Although I sometimes admire the technical virtuosity of well-wrought, complex designs, I am not moved to use them. I enjoy the process of reworking a design through several quilts, as I did with three quilts made using the Attic Window pattern to create an image of gardens.

When planning a quilt, I don't anguish over design, but choose one suitable to the scale of the work. Usually I draw it up on paper to see the secondary patterns which develop and to determine the proportions of the borders. I do this fairly roughly, shading the dark and medium values to see if I like the balance.

Colour is the most important element to me and it is the first thing that draws me to a quilt in an exhibition. Although I feel the

Morning Star by Margot Child. 232 cm x 232 cm (91½ in. x 91½ in.). Seminole machine pieced. Hand quilted. Traditional Eight-Point Star design

lack of artistic training, my use of colour has improved with trying. Gardens are my best source of inspiration — I love purples with reds and a splash of yellow with blues. When I have made enough blocks to see the design develop I throw them around on the bed and look hard to see what is lacking. Almost always it is either the complementary colour (usually yellow or orange) which adds life in small quantities, or darker values of colours that I have already used, which add depth and richness. The yellow print with its lacy design was vital to *Morning Star* both for its scale and colour. For me this stage is where the anguish is, and I don't hurry the process, but add and reject blocks until the overall effect pleases me.

Our youngest daughter is a relief printmaker and I often look to her for advice. We enjoy going to the Art Gallery, usually once a month, and always to major exhibitions, and I find this very stimulating as well as companionable. There are so many opportunities to see good design and colour use, and to be inspired in a big city like Sydney if you keep your eyes and your mind open.

Like all quilters, I love fabric and have a big collection — some scraps go back 40 years. I do buy fabric on impulse if it attracts me, although I might not use it straight away. Occasionally I'll buy three metres of something special for a border, but mostly I'll buy half a metre (18 in.), or 30 cm (12 in.) if it is expensive. I prefer the feel and needling quality of pure cotton and like it to be reasonably dense and fine. I look for a variety of scale in patterns and never buy selections of closely toned prints in one colour. I like to add English Liberty prints to my scrap quilts because they provide a wonderful intensity and variety of dyes and because of the timeless quality of their design. I have enough fabric to last me a lifetime — I'll have to live to 110 to use it all!

When cutting out prints, I seldom focus on the motif. But some prints have a lot happening in them and so I may try to extract elements for a particular effect. *Morning Star* was made using the seminole technique but two motifs needed to be centred, so the sewing took twice as long. I work slowly and don't mind how long it takes to get the result I want. Depending on the project, I machine or hand piece and I always handquilt. Where possible I use a low-loft batting because I like the flatter look, and the quilting is better integrated with the piecing. Old quilts have this flat look.

With busy scrap quilts I mostly outline the quilt to add dimension, but with a piece like *Morning Star* I work out a quilting design to suit the spaces. This particular one was developed from the paisley pattern in the border fabric to enhance the radiating effect of the star. I also use old traditional designs and

enjoy the feeling that they have been used by generations of women.

My aim is to make quilts which are pleasing to the eye, technically sound and worth the work that went into them. When I hear people say reverently "She spent 2000 hours on this quilt", I want to ask them, "But was it worth it?" If the design, colour and technique do not come together as a pleasing whole, we are wasting too many precious hours.

MARJORIE COLEMAN

I came under the thrall of quilts 18 years ago in Hawaii and while the magic remains, I have worked my way through doing all sorts of bed quilts and now no longer make them.

What excites me is to see a piece on a wall. Not a bed quilt on a wall but a piece designed to look at me, eye to eye, made for that plane and to that proportion. Not to cover a field of a wall, not to help the acoustics, not to boast how clever the owner was in some flea market, but to reach out in its own right, of its own self, shouldering aside the upstart paintings and photographs and

Marjorie Coleman

prints to call out: "This is where I am".

I think it is important to use one's own thoughts, the perceptions and loves of one's own time and place, rather than someone else's hand-me-downs; to use the past for the steps it can suggest, rather than for the provision of present substance. All the quilts I have made were explorations and, though I have never copied a quilt, my early ones were of my own design expressed in traditional techniques. They were quite successful and since I was using Australian native plants as my theme, before it became so fashionable, they attracted attention. But they were not my ultimate goal, though I knew that each one made was a step nearer to the radical and even outrageous concepts which I want to express. But it's a hard slog with my temperament. I was properly brought up by an English mother and that's a hard mask to shed. At times I fear that I am a generation too late.

I want to master technique and then forget it. When it is the *how* of the piece which first draws attention rather than the *what*, I feel that the piece is disappointing and will eventually pall. The same applies to poor technique. A design, colour, or fabric may be spectacular but if poor technique catches the eye first, it is not for my wall, although it may be fine for the baby to lie on.

I have tremendous struggles with colour. I usually find cartooning-out the quilt fairly uncomplicated and easy enough, even exciting, but interpreting that cartoon in its colours can leave me with a reeling head and filled with indecision. If, as I sometimes do, I start with a piece of fabric and develop the quilt

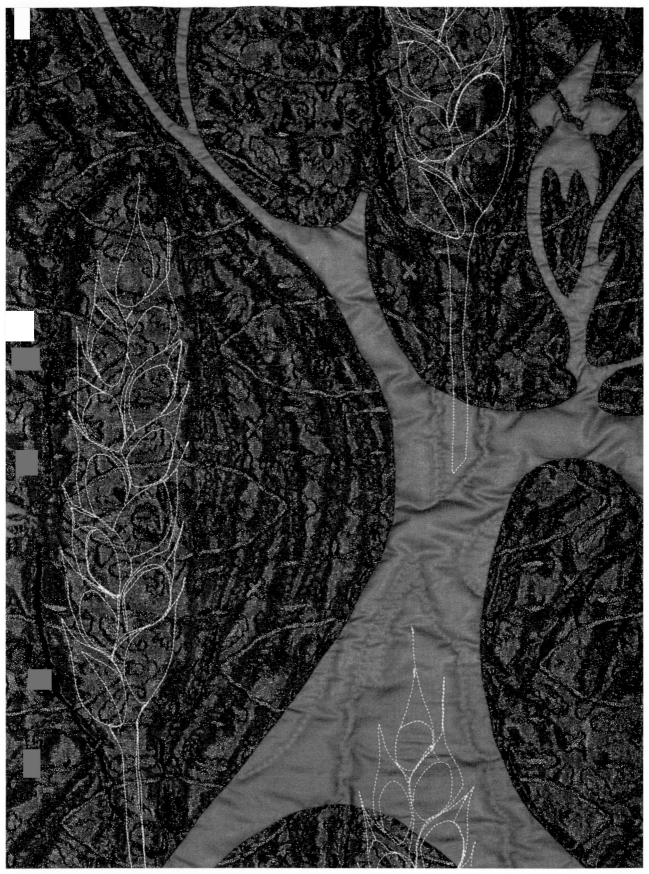

Momento Mori by Marjorie Coleman. 109 cm x 95 cm (43 in. x 37½ in.). Hand appliquéd and machine embroidered. Hand quilted

San Blas Study No. 2 by Marjorie Coleman. (Work in progress.) 44 cm x 58 cm (17 ½ in. x 23 in.). Reverse appliqué by hand

from it, I have much less trouble — perhaps that is why I do not respond to dyeing. Perhaps I need the security of something structured.

I have always used off-beat fabric. Indeed this is a big part of my interest in quilts, fitting in this and that, finding a piece with just the right colour, sometimes, in desperation, home dyeing, although this is not something I enjoy doing. Forcing commercial fabric to my purpose is much more exciting than dyeing or printing. Sometimes, however, a touch of something printed or dyed may be necessary to extend an effect but, like nudity on the stage, only if it is necessary to the story-line. I also suspect that there is hidden in me some fugitive neurosis which makes me think that dyeing is chickening out, yet I like it in the quilts of others. Strange.

So there is, for me, a constant tension between developing new ways to manipulate fabric, or learning new technology, and submerging it into what the piece is saying. The "gee whiz!" of technique must serve a further purpose. This is something I have only lately come to understand and the understanding has changed my direction.

I would like to make pieces which speak to people who are not interested in quilts, to use a quilter's insights and skills to lure those who dismiss quilts as largely busywork. This is a rather large ambition, perhaps even arrogant — I have a long way to go.

TRUDY BILLINGSLEY

Seventeen years ago, when Justin was a baby, I began quilting. I realised that I could not have a

Trudy Billingsley

full-time job and a family as well so I stayed at home. Until that time I had not done a lot of handwork apart from some weaving and needlepoint. I decided I would have to do something that satisfied me.

My early experiences have a strong influence on my work. Today, I look at my children and am reminded of how much you learn from your parents and environment. This is the source of a lot of my creativity. I never feel bored because I am always thinking of a new design.

My own children are becoming better observers. Today when we were shopping, my daughter Sally bought a postcard with a series of corrugated iron roofs. She looked at the colours and immediately thought of a design and I think that is probably the way I started with my parents. She is not frightened to observe and design, as she sees me doing it.

My mother was always making things and my father made me observe nature. "Look at that flower" and "Look at the colour of the sea today", he would say. A

lot of people brush by things but do not really see them. They walk around busy with what they are doing and they don't really see what is around them, especially in our landscape — the colours, the textures and the feelings they evoke.

What makes me interested in landscape is that there are so many different colours in the landscapes of various countries. When you return to Australia the clarity of our colours and our deep blue skies stand out. You just don't see skies as blue as ours anywhere else in the world.

I am really conscious of colours. Poor light bothers me, particularly dull days. If the light is not right it annoys me. I lived for a time in Boston and even the sunny days there have a soft, filtered light. This light softens colours and it made me miss the colours of our landscapes as rendered by our brilliant sunshine.

While I was living in Boston an American friend who had lived in Australia gave me a little piece of fabric tape from the "Keep

Snorkelling at Beaver Cay by Trudy Billingsley. 154 cm x 170 cm (60½ in. x 67 in.). Machine pieced. Hand appliquéd and quilted

Australia Beautiful" campaign. I thought, "I'll have to do a quilt — *Keep Australia Beautiful*" (not illustrated). I started to draw it up as a traditional quilt but it wouldn't come together. It was then I realised that I had to have more freedom in the design process. Nancy Halpern's work was a continuing inspiration at this time although her approach is geometric.

I decided to start drawing landscapes freehand and developed an easy piecing

method. This made me become interested in fabrics as landscape colours. If, for example, I found a fabric that had birds in it then I could use it for the sky. Contemporary printed fabrics that had a curve suggested the roll of a wave. I was also interested in overdyeing fabrics. I still love traditional work but I am more fulfilled by landscapes.

To begin a quilt I start by drawing up the cartoon, a full-sized design on paper pinned to a wall. I then trace off each piece,

using tracing paper as a template.

The fabrics that I have selected for the quilt are arranged on the floor and I choose each piece from this. Frequently a quilt is inspired by a particular collection of fabrics. I had been collecting fabrics for *Snorkelling at Beaver Cay* long before I started it. I kept thinking of aquas and bright tropical colours.

I begged and borrowed fabric because I had not done any pieces in those tropical colours before. I spoke to Wendy Holland, Helen

Macartney, and Margot Child to ask them if they had anything in those colours. I find it very interesting to ask someone for something tropical and then to see how they interpret it. I enjoy using other people's fabrics; it is fun when they look at my finished quilt and say, "I remember that piece". One's fabric stocks can eventually become limiting. If you use a fabric selection in one quilt and then in another and another, they all take on a sameness. It really is necessary to refresh your fabric stock.

Obviously some favourite bits get spread around a few quilts: I particularly enjoy putting bitsy things, like shiny fabrics, in quilts, especially in water and sunsets. They add life.

Holidays always inspire me, because I relax and have more time to observe. *Snorkelling at Beaver Cay* was inspired by a holiday at Dunk Island. I remember the magnificent colours of the fish and the water. We came home and it had been such a terrific experience that I felt I should record it.

I am at ease with the colours of water and I like working on images of water and leaves using the blues and greens. Primary colours are more difficult so it is quite a challenge to work with tropical colours. I do not feel at all comfortable with them. Sunset colours and the colours of the outback, like rusts and browns, are easy for me.

Making quilted landscapes is time consuming and can be tedious. Often the handquilting is difficult because you have to sew through many layers of fabrics, so I have started a Cloak in the Garden quilt to give myself a break. It's smaller than a landscape and I am using tropical colours to give myself more

Sashiko Teepee by Wendy Holland. 184 cm x 154 cm (72½ in. x 60½ in.). Machine pieced. Hand quilted

experience with them. I always complete one piece at a time, although I usually have one piece to quilt and one piece being finished at any one time. While I'm working on my main quilt I do small pieces like dropped-waist belts with strip piecing and collage.

Soon I will attend some more workshops on dyes and I am really interested in doing some more fabric creation. It will be fun and I always enjoy the stimulation. I have been to many different workshops that have nothing to do with quilting but my quilting always benefits.

I am very disciplined now and by 8.30 am I am in the workroom

that was built for me by my husband Geoff and my son Justin. I decide what I am going to do and stay there until it has been done. I never have too many things going at once.

WENDY HOLLAND

Because of my background training as a painter, I look at quilts as textile paintings, combining elements of shape, pattern and colour with the possibilities of unexpected juxtapositions created by the fabric medium.

I first saw old quilts during a

A Sea Change by Wendy Holland. 207 cm x 179 cm (81½ in. x 70½ in.). Screen-printed Ocean Waves pattern. Machine pieced. Hand quilted with crochet cotton

Ursine Offering by Wendy Holland. 232 cm x 196 cm (91½ in. x 77 in.). Screen-printed Bears Paw pattern. Machine pieced. Hand quilted

showcase for interesting, old or unusual fabrics though I like to disregard the traditional tonal formulas so that the block pattern is not too obvious.

A Sea Change, Pale Ladies (see page 146) and *Ursine Offering* all belong to a series of quilts loosely based on the shapes of simple, ethnic or folk garments. This garment reference is only a starting point and may become submerged or transformed as construction of the quilt progresses. *A Sea Change*, which includes Japanese and Indonesian fabrics, began with reference to Japanese happi coats. The lapels (with trade identification) also suggest a Shinto shrine or gateway (a feminine symbol) into an Eastern Garden of Eden.

Those mad Filipino puffed sleeves also appear in the top corners. The lower half of the quilt is made from a traditional Ocean Waves quilt pattern that I printed, assembled and cut up again. Hence "a sea change", from the well-known quote from *The Tempest*.

Pale Ladies started as a traditional medallion quilt. The fabric in the central panel joins together reproductions of a colonial American painting showing a lady in sprigged calico dress with three gents.

This quilt contains many old, pale and pretty fabrics including Japanese handkerchiefs. The overall arrangement refers to the shape of the lady's dress, with the randomly pieced lower half of the quilt suggesting a large fragmented triangle. With the apex upwards, the triangle is an earth or female symbol.

The diagonals that cut through each side repeat the sticks inserted through the Japanese ladies' hairdos. I like the combination of Japanese and

trip to England and was struck by the muted colours and curious prints as well as by the extensive use of stripes and checks. I had collected fabrics for years, including odd prints and Japanese kimonos, which had gone into clothes and various textile items, leaving lots of lovely bits and pieces.

My first quilts were very traditional in the English Medallion style. I planned the layout and then worked out which fabrics would go where, cut it all out with templates and joined it all up. In other words your design and creative decisions are all made before you sew a stitch.

I soon found I was more interested in starting with a particular collection of fabrics and playing around to make the most of these fabrics and their relationships to each other within the rectangular quilt format. For example, I enjoy cutting and joining striped material in different directions off the grain of the fabric, or randomly joining up various scraps and cutting up and rejoining.

Then again I might use a very simple formal or informal arrangement if the fabric suggests it such as in *Japanese Stripes* (see page 38) or *Java Quilt* (see page 114).

I will always have a fondness for these scrapbag quilts as a

American elements — East meets West. I made the quilt in 1986, the International Year of Peace — it seemed appropriate.

A North American Indian medicine man's deerhide costume, with quill-work and beaded decoration was the inspiration for *Ursine Offering*. I like the idea that a garment decorated with symbols and amulets has the property of endowing the wearer with magical powers or providing special protection. I also wanted to cut up and include a traditional Bear's Paw quilt — more triangles — I had printed and assembled. The American Indian connection combined with hidden or lost footprints seemed appropriate.

Incorporating the bordello fabric was a bit of a challenge. The lower part of the quilt ended up suggesting an altar attended by naked priestesses in a state of abandoned religious fervour.

This quilt was also very much an exercise in playing with colour. It contains a cross-cultural mix of fabrics, from pale old furnishing fabrics printed with mauve and blue sweet peas, to dark Japanese kasuri and tan Indonesian batiks.

My most recent quilts are becoming less symmetrical and more like abstract paintings. I still like putting together bits and pieces of fabrics from many different sources, and playing with colours, shapes and the break-up of space.

I enjoy the decorative and abstract relationships that are determined by the materials, and the construction process which allows me to cut it up and try again if I change my mind.

MARGARET ROLFE

I believe that an art form that does not change and evolve is a dying art form. While I enjoy the American pieced-block patterns based on regular grids, I wanted to add an Australian dimension, so I began with designs based on Australian wildflowers.

I did not want to be restricted to conventional patchwork shapes — the square, the triangle and the rectangle — that result from designing on a regular grid. But at the same time I did not want to design blocks that were impossible to sew. I then hit on the idea of straight-line piecing, in which every piece in a block joins together with a straight seam provided the piecing order is followed. To make the piecing order easier to follow, I gave every piece in the design a number, and wrote out the piecing order in steps.

Simplicity has always been one of my major aims in creating designs. My yardsticks are the Shoofly which has 13 pieces, and the Ohio Star which has 21 pieces. I now try to keep my designs within these limits, but it's not always possible. The aesthetic verdict is the final one.

I get my ideas from every-where. I have a head full of quilts I want to make. As for the design process, my scrapbooks are a major resource. I cut out and keep every picture that I like for any reason — for colour, line, subject or whatever. I have pages and pages of pictures of wildflowers, for instance, and also of pandas.

Specific designs often require research, though, and I have lots of reference books. I borrow from friends and libraries. Inspiration strikes in odd places, and I quickly scribble down the idea on whatever is handy. Drawing is an excellent preparation for designing, not because I am particularly good at drawing, but because it forces me to sit down and look at things very closely, and then to work out exactly what the shapes are and what relationships there are between these shapes.

My computer is another very important design tool, but I stress that it is just a tool. I still create the designs, the computer just makes it quicker and easier (for example, see Diagram 3 and photograph opposite). I use an Apple Macintosh, well known for its graphic capabilities and user friendliness. The drafting package is called Macdraw.

The screen has a grid on which I can determine the intervals, perhaps eight divisions to the inch or four to the centimetre. Having determined the grid the computer will then lock any lines or shapes that I draw into it so everything is totally accurate. Once a block or shape is drawn, I can flip it upside down or sideways, or rotate it. I can repeat the block or shape at the press of a single key. This is great for designing block-based quilts, because you can so easily play with the blocks and their placement. I can make the blocks or designs larger or smaller and I can also use patterns to shade in parts of the design and this helps with tonal values.

When I like what I have designed, I print out a copy onto a sheet of paper. I tape up the designs in the kitchen where I can look at them from a distance, and take account of any critical comments made by my family.

I think designing has to be ranked as my chief love. I enjoy sewing, but I could not possibly make all the quilts I design, so at times I have others make them for

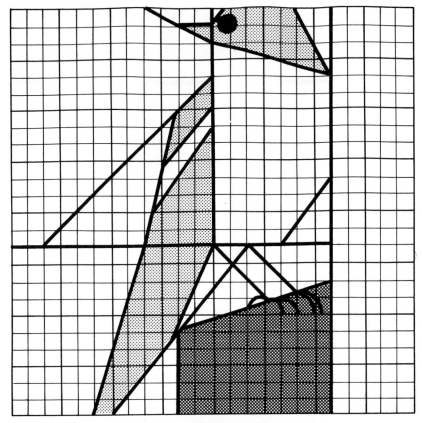

3 Block design of a Flame Robin by Margaret Rolfe: a straight piecing design

Flame Robin Block by Margaret Rolfe. 24 cm x 24 cm
(9½ in. x 9½ in.). Machine pieced. Hand quilted

me. I really enjoy seeing my designs creatively interpreted by different people.

DIANE DOWE

This montage (see page 54) is a photographic record of my collections, my influences and my work: old textiles, cotton, linen, silk and metallic embroidery threads, buttons, belts, beads, antique fabric motifs, period costume, ribbons, braids, lace and much more.

I have an obsession with visual stimulus — one object will trigger off a series of ideas. Then the way to achieve those ideas is through the most appropriate technique, perhaps through embroidery, or fabric collage, etching or mosaic work.

I have tried to create a visual idea of my world. The images around the edge of the montage are mostly the things that influence me and some of my collections (like buttons), while the central images show some of the diverse aspects of my work. There are some "initial" works in the montage. These were part of a self-imposed exercise to explore various techniques using the letters in my name. I made, for example, a denim "D" embroidered in satin stitch on stiff denim. For each stitch I had to drag the needle through the fabric with a pair of pliers. A petit point "E" shows 10,000 tiny stitches using pearl and metallic threads. There is a graphic "W" made with old "slope cards" in a collage on a marbled paper background.

Some of the larger works were carried out during a four-month stint in hospital. I was immobile and had no access to iron and fabrics, so I created a series of

Montage of works by Diane Dowe

Planning for *Fields* by Diane Dowe showing the design of aerial views of a formal garden with chosen fabrics and notions

four works with stitched, cut and torn papers, wrapped sticks, old fans, gold dust, silk and metallic threads, and handmade papers.

The central mosaic vessel is inspired by Crazy Patch and old blue and white damask tablecloths. The idea of working with blue and white china seemed a natural progression. The broken pieces of different china patterns are stuck together like crazy paving or crazy patchwork. The vessel is filled with embroidered felt balls. Together, the vessel and balls are sympathetic yet opposite, one heavy and sharp, the other soft and light.

The occasional hand-painted peg, screen-printed doll or piece of "button" jewellery pops out in the other works. I use amusing things like these to lighten my load.

ADÈLE OUTTERIDGE

The *Miniature Star* was worked with solid colours as a radiating design (see page 90). I wanted to keep the tones as close to each other as possible in a mid range. The darker border was not my original choice, but proved most successful.

Monkey Wrench (see page 56) is a favourite traditional design. I have worked it in several media. I wanted to use tone to give a feeling of advancing and receding. I started out with a large bundle of squares and triangles which I arranged so that the tones of the fabrics forming the grid were light compared to the rest of the design. Rather than keeping the tone of the triangles constant, I worked from dark to mid range, merging the tones of the background and the grid in one area, so that the background appears to advance to the same visual level as the grid.

I repeated the design using paint and discovered that paint cannot give the wonderful depth of colour of fabric. The woven texture gives a richness while the paint remains flat. Even six coats of acrylic could not match it.

When I am working I generally don't try to visualise the finished result — I spend a lot of time playing with pieces of fabric. This gives me far more freedom than paint. I can develop a more interesting and sophisticated colour scheme working with fabric (a particular example is *Monkey Wrench*.) The opportunity to manipulate the fabric allows all kinds of unusual things to happen, whereas when I use paint I don't always get the surprises. Once paint is laid down it is fixed, whereas pieces of fabric can be moved. Fabric stretches your ingenuity because you do not have a full palette. I do not dye fabric, rather I let the fabrics themselves suggest colour schemes, whereas with paint I work to a proven colour system.

Those quick quilts that can be run up in a day or two may be appealing, but are not necessarily heirlooms. They are great for the children to jump on and for the cat and dog to lie on. They may be charming, and in years to come when they have faded, they may be praised for the mellowness of age, but that still does not necessarily make them great quilts. Quilts that have taken hundreds of hours are not necessarily all masterpieces either. The number of hours spent in construction or the cost of the fabric do not always make a masterpiece. Rather the colours, design and construction must work.

I have made a series of books to use as resource files. Everything goes into these books, they contain all my reference material. Whenever I have an idea, I jot it

Monkey Wrench by Adèle Outteridge. 103 cm x 103 cm (40½ in. x 40½ in.). Machine pieced. Hand quilted

down, make a little sketch and keep it filed. I also keep cuttings, photographs, leaves, shells, bark, gumnuts and so forth.

Fabric manipulation is an extension of playing around with the colour of fabrics — one thing leads to another (see pages 122–23). You might start off with one idea but then your mind does a lateral jump and the design develops in a different direction. I generally work on a flat surface. Everything gets turned upside down and on its side. I look at the pieces from every possible direction. I have found that some things will often look better on the back than on the front. I frequently use the backs of fabrics because they can look more interesting. I have also found that the raw, exposed edges of seams work well when I turn a piece over and feature the back of the work.

Photography is another of my interests. Sometimes I combine photography with textiles. In one piece I used an old picture of myself and layers of transparent fabric. I stitched grid lines through the stack and then cut through the fabrics, turning them back to reveal glimpses of the photograph. As the fabrics were turned back, the levels of transparency changed, adding depth.

In another piece I enlarged a photograph of water reflections and photocopied it onto overhead projection film. I layered the film with fabrics in black and white, and it became an exercise in texture. I once used scrunched up tarlatan which came from the printmakers' waste.

I am also interested in space dyeing (dropping ink onto wet fabric). Some of the results were a bit disappointing until I started scrunching up the space-dyed fabric. Suddenly I had colour contrasts and colour reactions. Interesting things started to happen. I gathered, folded, and pleated the strips. The final result was the fans (see page 121). I also love to experiment with torn, cut and frayed edges. On another occasion I was tying silk (knotting a layer of silk together with the batting and lining). The needle was blunt and pulled the threads, creating rows of lines connecting the ties.

There are so many avenues to explore, so many possibilities present themselves with fabric manipulation. The samples illustrated in the chapter on Fabric Manipulation provide an introduction to possibilities beyond traditional quiltmaking.

Quilt on bed: *Pink Sampler* by Elizabeth Ashley. 250 cm x 210 cm (98½ in. x 82½ in.). Hand pieced, appliquéd and quilted. Crazy Patch quilt c. 1940s folded on end of bed. Maker unknown. Evening bag by Jocelyn Campbell. On quilt stand: folded appliqué quilt by Marjorie Patterson and folded stripped quilt by Mary Hinde

QUILT CONSTRUCTION

Requirements for drafting, cutting and sewing a quilt. Workbox by Ann-Marie Bakewell, pincushion by Wendy Saclier and Vivienne Mildren, supplies by *Patchwork and Primitives*, Willoughby.

PREPARATION

SUPPLIES FOR SEWING THE QUILT TOP

Thread Thread compatible with the fabric. Polycotton blends work well. Grey and light brown are useful. For appliqué you must match the thread to the top fabric. Quilting thread.

Scissors Good scissors for fabric (I recommend Ginghers). Another pair for cutting paper.

Rotary Cutter The larger the better. Spare blades.

Cutting Mat For use with the rotary cutter.

Needles No. 7 to No. 9 betweens for quilting (the smaller the better). You may like sharps or fine crewel needles for sewing.

Thimble To fit the middle finger of the sewing hand. Metal with indentations. A leather thimble is an alternative.

Pins Fine, long pins are best (e.g. Newey lace pins).

Ruler A metal ruler is best, preferably 60 cm (24 in.) long. Any long ruler with undented edges is acceptable.

Gridded Ruler Perspex with the smallest intervals available.

Pencils HB, 6B. Plus a sharpener. A silver pencil is useful for work on dark fabrics.

Fabric See the following sections.

Seam Ripper To unpick stitches.

Felt Square To lay out pieces in a block for hand sewing. Store the felt rolled up.

Iron and Ironing Board A good steam iron.

Sewing Machine Optional.

PLANNING THE QUILT

Most quilts are carefully planned: the design is chosen and drawn out to scale, templates of each shape are made, and all the pattern pieces are cut and then sewn together in an orderly sequence. When the top is complete it is basted to the batt and lining, and the quilting line sewn. Finally, the edges are finished.

To start, choose a pattern that suits your level of experience. Easier patterns have fewer pieces in them, so if you are just starting out avoid too many bias edges, curves, long, tapered points and set-in corners.

If you are designing a quilt to fit a specific bed, the dimensions of the quilt must first be established. Diagram 4 shows the measurements to be taken. To arrive at the length of the quilt, measure the length of the bed, and add the drop, which may be about 45 cm (18 in.) The quilt should not drag on the floor or it will wear quickly. Add an allowance for a pillow tuck, about

20 cm (8 in.) is usually enough. To calculate the width, measure across the bed and add the length of two drops (down both sides of the bed). Allow about 5 cm (2 in.) both ways to allow for the shrinkage caused by quilting. Now you have the overall dimensions of the quilt (see Table opposite).

Next, consider the size and arrangement of blocks (if that is your proposed design) in the quilt. Decide if the blocks are to sit on the point or not, and work out the number of blocks that fit across the bed and down the length. This is called the set of the quilt. Diagrams 5a, b and c on page 62 show different arrangements. Draw the block in miniature, about 2.5 cm (1 in.) across, and photostat many copies. Play with these blocks, arranging them in different sets, with or without a lattice, until you find the arrangement that pleases you most. If you spray a fabric adhesive on the back of the photostat blocks before you cut them up, they will stick to the paper that you lay them down on, but can be easily peeled off and rearranged. If there are sashes

4 Measuring for a bed quilt

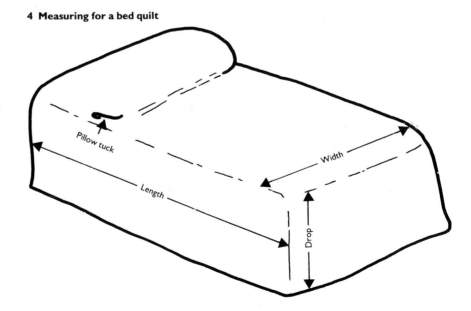

Common block arrangements (or sets)

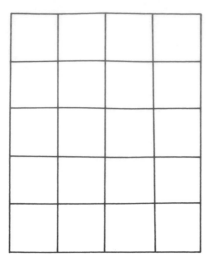

5a Straight set

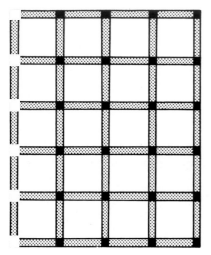

5b Straight set with lattice and
isolated corners

5c Pieced blocks on the point
alternating with plain blocks

CALCULATING THE SIZE OF A BED QUILT

Standard mattress sizes:

	cm	in.		cm	in.
Cot	130 × 70	52 × 27	Queen	205 × 150	80 × 60
Single	190 × 100	75 × 39	King	205 × 195	80 × 76
Double	190 × 135	75 × 54			

Single bed example:

Quilt size

To calculate the quilt size for a single bed with a drop of 45 cm (18 in.) including the 5 cm (2 in.) shrinkage factor:

$$\text{Length} = \binom{190 \text{ cm}}{75 \text{ in.}} \text{mattress length} + \binom{20 \text{ cm}}{8 \text{ in.}} \text{pillow tuck} +$$

$$\binom{45 \text{ cm}}{18 \text{ in.}} \text{drop} + \binom{5 \text{ cm}}{2 \text{ in.}} \text{shrinkage factor} = \frac{260 \text{ cm}}{103 \text{ in.}}$$

$$\text{Width} = \binom{100 \text{ cm}}{39 \text{ in.}} \text{mattress width} + 2\binom{45 \text{ cm}}{18 \text{ in.}} \text{drop} +$$

$$\binom{5 \text{ cm}}{2 \text{ in.}} \text{shrinkage factor} = \frac{195 \text{ cm}}{77 \text{ in.}}$$

Fabric requirements:

Lining — just over twice the length = 5.50 m (6 yd)

Top — either calculate each fabric as shown, or allow twice the lining (i.e. 11 m or 12 yd) as a general guide for a pieced top. Appliqué will need a background fabric the same as the lining plus different fabrics for the appliquéd shapes.

Once you have decided on the block pattern and size, consider the placement of fabrics. If the same combination of fabrics are to be used in all the blocks it is possible to calculate the yardage you will need. If you plan to make a scrap quilt, however, it is more difficult to work out the required yardage because some fabrics may work out better than others, so the quantity of each cannot be easily determined.

separating the blocks, remember to include them. If the numbers do not fit comfortably into the required quilt size, you can adjust (or add) a border design to fill out extra space. As the side borders can vary from the bottom border, and the top ones can even be eliminated, there is plenty of room for adjustment to fit into the final dimensions. Diagram 6 illustrates elements of the quilt. This diagram (see page 64) is based on *Carly's Quilt* by Susan McIver (page 65).

An all-over design that covers the whole quilt is another possible arrangement. In this case it can be drawn to fit the surface area of the quilt. Rather than stick together dozens of sheets of paper, used computer printout or ends of newspaper rolls, or even rolls of photographic paper that have

7 Cutting layout for appliqué

8 Fabric grain

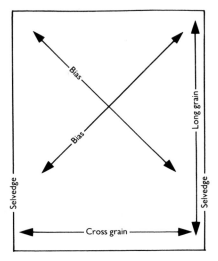

been discarded are very useful. Marking the design with a water-soluble felt-tip pen on very wide sheets of plastic makes the design process easier because the lines can be rubbed out easily. Most quilts, however, are based on blocks that are repeated.

To work out the yardage of a block quilt, first study the pieces in one block and decide how many of each shape are required in each fabric. Multiply this by the number of blocks in the quilt. Taking into account that each shape has a seam allowance of 5 mm ($\frac{1}{4}$ in.), calculate how many of a particular shape will fit across the width of the fabric (this is usually 115 cm [45 in.]). Work out how many rows you will need to cut and multiply this by the number of pieces of a particular kind in a row, to give the total number of pieces required. You know how deep each row is, so multiply this measurement (again adding seam allowance) by the number of rows and you have the quantity needed of that fabric.

Repeat this exercise for each shape in every fabric, as well as sashes and borders. Some people prefer not to have a join in their borders, in which case you will need to buy enough fabric for the full length of the border, even though there may be considerable wastage.

Isolating features or stripes means that extra fabric must also be allowed. Always buy a little more in any case to allow for

shrinkage or mistakes, or a change of mind.

The amount of fabric required for an appliqué quilt is harder to estimate accurately because the shapes do not tessellate like the squares, triangles, diamonds and other shapes of pieced work. But some of the same rules still apply. Consider the various shapes and imagine each in a box. If the same shape recurs often, then there will be rows of these "boxes", which may be squares, rectangles or triangles (Diagram 7). By nesting the boxes in these rows, it is possible to calculate how many of each shape will fit across a width of fabric, and how many rows will be necessary. The length of each row multiplied by the number of rows will give the yardage. Always buy extra.

Unlike piecing, appliqué is laid on a background fabric, so enough of this fabric (often cream or white, to show up the appliqué) to cover the area of the quilt top must be purchased. It can be joined in the same manner as the lining (see diagram 70b on page 134).

Hawaiian Appliqué requires two layers of fabric, each of which may also be seamed before cutting them out.

GRAINLINE

In general, the fabric grain line for all patterns should run in the same direction so that the finished quilt has the long grain (Diagram

8) running the length of the quilt. This is the strongest and most consistent arrangement. However, several factors may lead you to abandon this rule. If a feature of the fabric is being selected, such as a flower or a stripe, this consideration will override grain line. Also, if wastage is a problem, or quick cutting techniques are preferred, then the direction of the grain may be overlooked.

If possible, ensure that the pieces around the edge of the block are on a straight grain because putting bias edges there could result in stretching through handling. A beginner may prefer to avoid sewing bias edges together for the same reason and may decide therefore to place the straight grain against bias.

COLLECTING FABRIC

Calculations for fabric needed for a specific quilt may not be so daunting if you have a large collection of fabric on hand. There are many justifications for buying fabric for your collection. If you are buying all the fabric for one quilt at the same time, you are at the mercy of the fashion of the day. The advantage of this is that a coordinated look is possible, but the exciting chance effects that can be created by combining fabrics from different periods is not. Also, if you have planned your quilt on graph paper with coloured pencils and then take this plan to match fabrics, the chances are that you will be disappointed by the range available.

A store of fabrics can act as an inspiration. You can play with combinations that you have on hand for a long time and then fill in the gaps with specially purchased fabric. A new project can be speedily started because you have enough fabric to go on with. The danger is, of course, that you might not have enough of the one fabric that is apparently indispensable. Do not be put off, fabric shortages have led to some of the most creative solutions and the quilt can be even better than you had hoped.

Do not forget that fabric shops are not the only source. Remnants from sewing projects by non-quilting friends, opportunity shops, outdated samples from interior design shops, stalls and garage sales can all turn up finds. When a friend offers to buy you something on a trip, ask for fabric — it is a revelation to find out what they think you like! The unexpected can be just the fabric that makes the statement you need. When purchasing fabric bear in mind your stock on hand. Unless you always work in a restricted range, such as all solids, make sure you vary the print sizes, colour and value. Include some fabrics you hate — they can zing up an otherwise bland quilt!

Storing the fabric can become a problem. The linen press is a good

6 Elements of the quilt A diagram based on *Carly's Quilt* by Susan McIver

starting place, but it can become obvious how much you have when you need yet another system of wire baskets. I have heard of one woman who put floorboards across the rafters in the ceiling. No one suspected how much she had. The fabrics should not be exposed to extremes of heat, to sunlight or moths. With a collection comes a real commitment to make quilts because there is no point in just buying it.

All fabric should be washed before storage. Then if you need something in a hurry you know that it can be used immediately. I do not iron it then because it will need pressing anyway to remove creases when it is used.

Washing is necessary for two reasons. Some fabrics, especially pure cotton, shrink with washing. Cotton shrinks by about three per cent, so it is best to eliminate the problem before it is sewn into a quilt top.

The other potential problem is bleeding. Some fabrics are not colour fast, particularly red, burgundy and navy blue.

To avoid the disaster of bleeding when the quilt is washed, test for colour fastness when the fabric is purchased. Light fabrics are probably safe and can be washed together, but any suspect fabric should be washed alone. Check the washing water for colour and rub the wet fabric with some white cloth and

Carly's Quilt by Susan McIver. 266 cm x 222 cm (104½ in. x 87½ in.). Hand and machine pieced. Hand appliquéd and quilted. Sampler

see if any colour comes out. If it does, wash and rinse the fabric several times, renewing the water each time, until the bleeding stops. If it continues to lose colour, return it to the shop you purchased it from and ask for your money back.

I always wash the fabric harder than I would the quilt, then I know that it can stand up to that treatment. I use ordinary washing detergent and a standard washing cycle on the machine. Naturally, if I am using non-traditional fabrics, such as velvets and silks, for a quilt that will hang on the wall and never be subjected to washing, I eliminate this step.

HAND OR MACHINE?

The decision to sew by hand or machine often depends on the temperament of the quiltmaker. For some, part of the joy is the handwork, allowing time for consideration of the placement of fabrics, as well as time to think about anything under the sun. The work can be taken anywhere, sewn while watching television, out with friends, by the bedside of a sick person, or at a meeting. I have even heard of someone sewing in the car at traffic lights, but this seems a little extreme.

The work can be taken up for a few minutes or for a long session.

Machine sewing is a less sociable activity because you are tied to the machine and if it has to be put away between sewing sessions there is less inclination to fill in short spaces of time with sewing. One of the obvious advantages of working on the sewing machine is the speed with which the quilt comes together. If you are keen to explore different colour and design possibilities, then the machine will allow you to accomplish more.

The final products of hand and machine piecing are indistinguishable, although the machine stitch is sturdier. Appliqué is a different matter because the stitch in hand appliqué can be almost invisible, whereas the machine stitch, whether straight stitching or satin stitch, lies on top of the fabric and is immediately visible, so it becomes part of the design.

Hand and machine quilting also give very different results. The running stitch of hand-quilting gives a much softer effect, and the opportunity to show off very small, even stitches, or long stitches in thicker thread if this is the desired effect. Machine stitching gives a harder line, and is less suited to many intricate, regular quilting patterns. Quilting in the ditch (along the seam lines) hides the machine stitch, and could be a quick solution.

Machine quilting is more practical for long lines of unbroken stitching or for more freeform quilting where the needle is used as a pencil to scribble on the pattern rather than carefully follow an intricate design. Intricate patterns are possible in straight stitching on the machine, but remember that for every turn in the design, the bulk of the quilt has to be swung under the head of the machine.

The choice of technique is a personal one, depending on preference and the desired effect. The same quiltmakers could choose one or the other form depending on the quilt and their commitments. There is no right answer, as long as the top and quilt design are considered when choosing the technique. Perhaps you could have one top being pieced on the machine while the last quilt is being handquilted. A cot quilt that is likely to be frequently in the wash might be machine pieced and quilted while the family heirloom could be entirely hand stitched. A quilt made to hang on a wall that will only be seen from a distance might well be sewn entirely by machine.

PIECING

Pieced quilts, composed of small shapes cut out in several fabrics and sewn together in a design, are still the most popular form of quiltmaking. If the whole surface of the quilt is subdivided into a single, recurring shape such as a square, triangle or hexagon, it is known as a one-patch. Most quilts, however, are subdivided into large squares that contain a pieced pattern. This square is known as a block. The block pattern is classified by the grid on which the block is based. (For some traditional block patterns, see page 161.)

The blocks are classified by the number of divisions along each side (Diagram 9): a four-patch block has four squares down by four across, so that the block is divided into 16 equal squares.

Similarly, five- and seven-patch blocks have 25 and 49 squares respectively. Strangely, though, a block that comprises a grid of three by three is termed a nine-patch. Each of these blocks can be subdivided further, so a 64-patch falls in the four-patch category, each side having eight equal divisions.

Unlike most pieced blocks, stars are not drafted on a grid. Eight-Point Stars and patterns based on their drafting, such as Castle Keep, are more common than stars with five or six points because more design possibilities arise from them.

Another category is drafted around an isolated central square. Log Cabin is the best known of these. There are some patterns that do not fit into any of these general categories and follow rules peculiar to that block. Feathered Star and Double Wedding Ring are both special (and complex) cases whose drafting is unique to them.

The arrangement of the blocks and their set (or layout) can be varied in many ways, giving rise to enormous design potential. The blocks may be all the same, or a pieced block may be alternated with a plain block or with another differently pieced block. In my quilt, *Red Cross* (see page 89), I used the large floral fabric from the alternating nine-patch block; this makes the edges of the block blur and the alternating blocks read as an irregular octagon rather than a square. By

9 Classification of blocks by grid

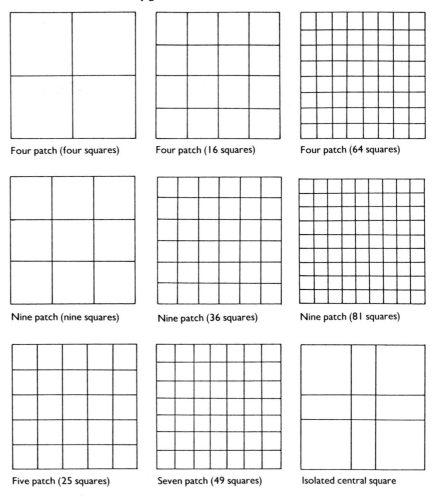

Four patch (four squares) Four patch (16 squares) Four patch (64 squares)

Nine patch (nine squares) Nine patch (36 squares) Nine patch (81 squares)

Five patch (25 squares) Seven patch (49 squares) Isolated central square

Kate's Quilt by Adèle Outteridge. 240 cm x 200 cm (94 in. x 78½ in.). Hand pieced and quilted

Hello Sonia by Adèle Outteridge. 180 cm x 180 cm (71 in. x 71 in.). Machine pieced.

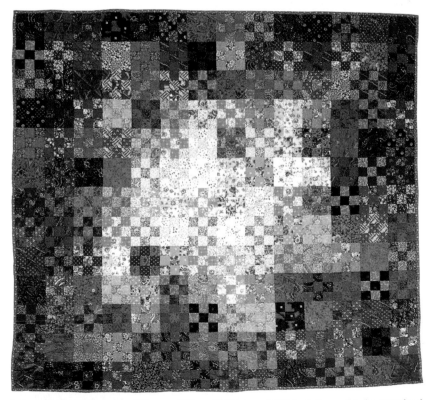

Autumn by Pam Timmins. 151 cm x 171 cm (59½ in. x 67½ in.). Some fabrics overdyed and tea dyed. Machine strip pieced. Hand quilted

continuing the triangle of floral fabric into the border, a huge square on the point develops across the quilt. The total design therefore seems more complex than the piecing design on which it is based. In *Kate's Quilt*, Adèle Outteridge alternates the Castle Wall pattern (which is derived from the drafting for an Eight Point Star) with a Mexican Cross. Once again a lattice appears because the eye extends the diagonal lines in the Mexican Cross into a lattice.

On the other hand, every block may be different. The sample quilt, in which this arrangement occurs, is a useful learning exercise and is often among the first quilts made by a beginner.

The blocks may be juxtaposed (as in *Hello Sonia* by Adèle Outteridge) or separated by sashes which build up into a lattice. Each block is enclosed by a narrow border and these borders unite into a lattice over the whole surface of the quilt. The blocks may be set horizontally or on their point. By rotating some blocks through 45° a feeling of movement can be achieved because many of the calming horizontal lines are replaced by diagonals.

The group of blocks may be surrounded by one or more borders. The borders can be plain fabric or may themselves be pieced, usually in a design relating to the blocks. An extension of this is the medallion quilt, which usually has a central block surrounded by a series of borders.

The choice of a solid or print fabric, and the decision whether to use the same fabrics throughout a quilt top, as Trudy Billingsley does with *Maple Leaf* (see page 27), or to vary them from block to block, can make two quilts look very different, even if the same pattern has been used. Changing the placement of light, medium and dark fabrics also adds complexity; the edges of the block can appear to lose definition. Pam Timmins has used this effect in *Autumn* (see page 67) by reversing her light and dark fabrics. To work out the arrangement, she threw all the blocks into the air and sewed them all more or less in the order that they came to rest.

SUPPLIES

Paper Larger than the finished block size.

Pencils HB, 4B, silver.

Ruler Metal or clear plastic as these will not be damaged by a rotary cutter. If patchwork is your passion it is worth buying rulers of different lengths, ranging from 15 cm (6 in.) to a metre (yard). If you purchase only one, a 60 cm (24 in.) is useful.

Square The 15 in. plastic square with a $\frac{1}{8}$ in. grid is useful. Metric squares (for example 40 cm) are less readily available. A large set square is an alternative. A 15 cm

(6 in.) square is useful for smaller shapes.

Bow Compass One with a central wheel for adjusting width. A beam compass with extension arm is occasionally useful, but not essential.

Protractor One measuring 360° (seldom needed).

Template Material Stiff, plastic film, preferably not opaque. Used X-ray film, the lid of a shirt box, or the side of a plastic milk container are very handy to use.

Felt-tip Marker Permanent, with a fine point. For marking template plastic.

Zip-lock Plastic Bags Useful for storing templates for a particular block.

DRAFTING BLOCKS WITH REGULAR GRIDS

Having chosen the block pattern and decided on its size, the next step is to draft up the block so that templates can be made of each shape. It is likely that the block size you require will not fit onto available graph paper, so it is useful to learn how to draft a square and develop a grid, dispensing with the need for graph paper altogether. Accuracy is essential in drafting your blocks, so it is worthwhile investing in good equipment.

DRAFTING THE BLOCK

Make the construction lines very light and thin (Diagram 10). Place the ruler near the bottom of the paper to draw a line of the required length (10a). Angle the pencil away from the ruler and tilt in the direction in which you are

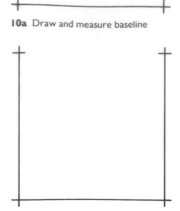

Drafting a square

10a Draw and measure baseline

10b Draw perpendiculars. Measure appropriate lengths along them

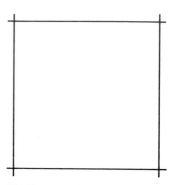

10c Connect points across top. Check lengths and angles (should be 90°)

drawing. Without moving the ruler, hold the square firmly against the ruler, with the vertical edge at the starting point. Draw the perpendicular then mark the length of the line required. Flip the square so that the maximum length rests along the first line. Draw another vertical line the required length from the end point of the first line (10b). Then join the lines across the top (10c). To check for accuracy, measure the last (top) line and check that the angles formed are right angles.

DRAFTING THE GRID

Having completed the square (say, 40 cm or 15 in.), the next step is to draft the grid. Here is an example based on a nine-patch.

Choose a number on your ruler into which three divides evenly, say, 45 cm (18 in.), and position the ruler with zero on the left hand bottom corner (point 0) of the square and the 45 cm (18 in.) mark on the right hand perpendicular side of the square. Holding the ruler firmly in position, mark the 15 cm (6 in.) and 30 cm (12 in.) points from the ruler onto the square. Half circle these points so that they are clearly visible (Diagram 11a). Place the plastic gridded square or set square on the block with its edge on the base line, then draw a perpendicular through the marked point. Repeat for the other point (11b). Next, rotate the paper through 90° and, using the new base line, repeat the procedure to construct the other set of perpendiculars (11c). Alternatively you can place the straight edge of a piece of paper against the bottom line, and transfer the end points and

intersections to the paper. The paper is then lined up against the other two sides, matching the end points, and the intersections can be transferred. Join the points on opposite sides to complete the grid.

Once the grid is constructed (11d), mark in the design lines of the chosen block in darker pencil so that these lines are stronger than the construction lines (11e).

TEMPLATES

After the block is drafted, examine it closely to find the intersection of lines that is most precise. Use this portion of the block to draft all templates. By using contiguous shapes, any small inaccuracies are likely to cancel each other out. The following instructions have been given for hand and machine piecing and for multilayer cutting.

HAND PIECING

Once you have decided how to approach the grain, place your template plastic over the block and transfer the shapes using a sharp HB pencil or a fine, permanent felt-tip marker. Number each pattern piece on the master draft of the block and on the template indicating the pattern name, the number of the pattern piece, the number of pieces required in each colour, and, if applicable, the number of pieces required in mirror image, as well as the preferred grain line. Cut apart the shapes in plastic using your scissors or a craft knife.

MACHINE PIECING

Templates for machine piecing include the seam allowance because when the edge of the presser foot is aligned with the edge of the fabric, the stitching line will be a seam-allowance

Drafting a Grid

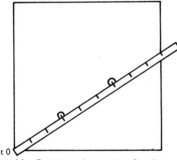

11a Position ruler at point 0 and rotate to meet righthand perpendicular at appropriate distance

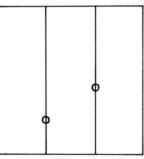

11b Mark in regular multiples for grid on block. Drop perpendiculars through points.

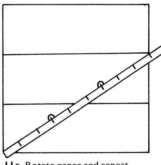

11c Rotate paper and repeat Steps 11a and b

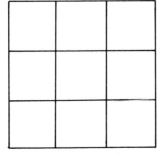

11d Construction lines of completed grid

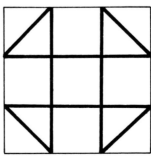

11e Transfer design lines of chosen block to grid

width in. So each pattern piece needs to have 5 mm ($\frac{1}{4}$ in.) added to each side.

MULTILAYER CUTTING

Rather than cutting out each shape individually, it is quicker to cut rows of some shapes in several layers of fabric. Squares and triangles are easy shapes (Diagram 12). The shape must include seam allowance, even for hand-sewn pieces. Individual templates are not necessary unless the work is being hand sewn, in which case the template is needed to trace the sewing lines onto the cut pieces.

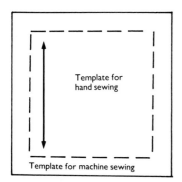

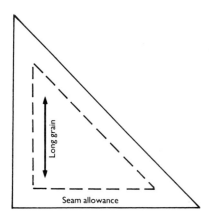

12 Templates for square pieces and triangular pieces showing seam allowances

MARKING AND CUTTING

Fabric should be washed and pressed before cutting. Next, remove the selvedges. Before cutting out the whole quilt, cut and sew a sample block to ensure that no errors have been made and that the effect is pleasing. The following instructions have been given for hand and machine piecing and multilayer cutting.

HAND PIECING

Position the template on the wrong side of the fabric so that the grain lines match up (see diagram 13). If possible mark up enough pieces for the whole quilt because it is quicker to complete all the cutting in one session, and it soon establishes whether or not you have sufficient fabric.

Arrange the shapes across the fabric so that they nestle into rows or blocks. This will leave you with a minimum of wastage. If a feature of a print is being highlighted, however, this technique is not possible.

Trace around the template carefully with a sharpened 4B pencil, although a silver pencil may show up better on dark fabric. Using the full length of the blade of the scissors, cut out the

shape allowing a 5 mm ($\frac{1}{4}$ in.) seam allowance on each edge.

MACHINE PIECING

Because the templates include seam allowances (12), they can be abutted. Otherwise, follow the guidelines for hand piecing above. Since the sewing line is measured in from the cutting line during piecing, it is vital that you cut out accurately because any small errors will accumulate as the pieces are joined and the finished work may not make the desired size or sit flat.

MULTILAYER CUTTING

Depending on the number of pieces you need and the number of fabrics involved, stack the pile of fabrics, aligning the long-grain edges. A fabric can be folded several times so that several layers of it are stacked. It may be necessary to fold each fabric lengthwise if the cutting mat is not very wide or if the ruler only measures 60 cm (24 in.). Carefully flatten out any wrinkles, otherwise they will be incorporated into the cut shapes, then top the stack with a light fabric because this will display the cutting lines clearly. Because these lines will disappear as you cut through them, they can be

13 Cutting layout for squares and right-angle triangles

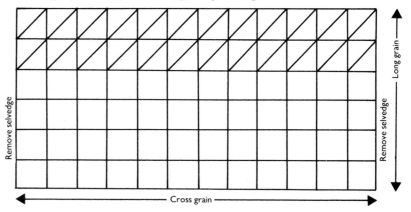

marked on the right or wrong side of the fabric.

No templates are used for cutting out shapes with this technique. Using a long ruler (preferably a yardstick) and a fine, permanent marker, draw up the rows of shapes to be cut out across the width of the fabric. A plastic ruler with a grid can be used to draft directly onto the fabric. If the fabric is to be cut by scissors, the number of layers is limited by the quality of the scissors — about eight layers is probably the maximum. To restrict any movement of the fabric, stab pin the shapes, but not too close to the cutting lines. Push the pin in at right angles to the stack of fabric so that it stabs the stack. If you push the pin in and out of the fabric in the normal manner it will distort the lower layers. And try to disturb the layers as little as possible while you cut.

If you plan to use a rotary cutter and mat, the number of layers can be increased to 12 or 16. No pins are needed using this method because the fabric will not be lifted by the cutter. If drafting directly onto the fabric use a ruler with a rubber or cork back so that it won't slip on the fabric. The wide plastic grids on the ruler will also anchor the fabric well. It may be necessary to fold each fabric lengthwise if the cutting mat is not very wide or if the ruler only measures 60 cm (24 in.).

First cut rows, then squares, and then triangles.

SEWING

THE ORDER OF PIECING

Analyse the block to determine the order of piecing. The aim is to build up triangles into squares

Order of piecing

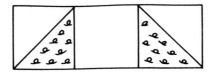

14a Join triangles to form squares

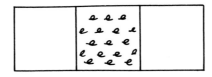
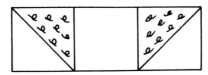
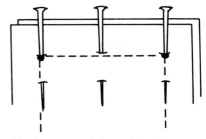

14b Join squares into rows

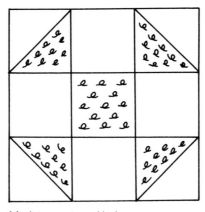

14c Join rows into a block

(Diagram 14a) and then into rows (14b), and then rows into blocks (14c), so that long lines of sewing are possible, and so that it is unnecessary to sew into corners. It is usual to sew one block at a time, which initially is satisfying. For speed, it is possible to take an assembly line approach. The same combination of pieces can be sewn for each block in the quilt, so that each operation is duplicated. Although this is not

immediately satisfactory, the final steps are exciting as whole sections of the quilt top come together. The latter technique is particularly suited to machine piecing.

HAND PIECING

Lay out the pieces in the order of the block on a felt square. This way it is easy to work out the sewing order. The fabric adheres to the felt so it can all be rolled up for storage or transportation. To begin, place the right sides together, matching the sewing lines, and pin the corners (Diagram 15a). This is a straightforward exercise for squares, but with the acute angles in triangles the seam allowance extends 5 mm ($\frac{1}{4}$ in.) beyond, so the pins must pass through the intersection of the sewing lines on both fabrics (Diagram 15b). On a long edge, pin through the sewing lines several times.

Pinning pieces for sewing

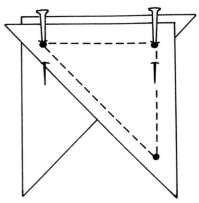

15a For squares, pin baste right sides together, matching corners and sewing lines

15b For triangles, match intersections of sewing lines

Choose thread that blends with the colour of the fabrics — a medium brown or grey generally works. Use a sharp ordinary needle or a crewel needle — the thinner the better — although some people do prefer to use their quilting betweens all the time. A between is a very short needle that facilitates small stitches. A thimble on the middle finger of the sewing hand helps push the needle through the fabric.

Thread the needle from the recently cut end of the thread and pull this end through the eye to knot it (Diagram 16). This ensures that the barbs of the thread lie down as they are passed through fabric, reducing knotting. To knot the end of the thread, pass the thread around the needle about four times and, holding the wrapped thread in place, pull the needle through. Keep pulling it until the knot forms at the end of the thread.

Sew from one end of the sewing line to the other, using a running stitch (Diagram 17). Load the needle with stitches and backstitch at the beginning of each needleful to increase the strength of the sewing. End the

16 Knotting the thread

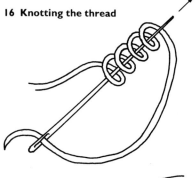

17 Running stitch

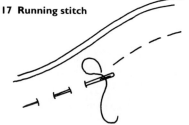

Sewing across seam allowances

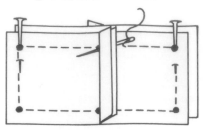

18a To hand sew crossed seams, pin securely, then backstitch at each intersection before and after seam allowance to leave seams free

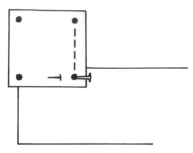

18b To sew inset corners, backstitch into corner, then rotate top piece to align with next edge and backstitch again

line of sewing with a backstitch or knot. Make sure you sew just inside the sewing line so that the thread is not made dirty by the lead pencil sewing line. This also corrects the minimal error created by tracing around the template.

Seams which cross over (Diagram 18a) should have been pinned securely to ensure that they match. Backstitch as you reach each intersection, then pass the needle through the fabric to the next piece, backstitching again through the exact intersection of the seam lines. This ensures that the corners meet crisply and that they will not gape. The seam allowance is left free to be pressed later in the most appropriate direction.

Although it is not very difficult to sew into corners, try to avoid it. If it *is* unavoidable, backstitch as you would with a crossed seam, passing the needle through exactly the same hole for the end of one seam line and the beginning of the next (18b).

MACHINE PIECING

Most machines have a presser foot 5 mm ($\frac{1}{4}$ in.) wide, so by aligning the edge of the fabric with the presser foot edge, the needle will sew leaving an appropriate seam allowance. If not, use the seam guide on the foot plate, or, if necessary, measure and tape a home-made seam guide onto the plate.

In machine piecing, seams are sewn from fabric edge to fabric edge, through the seam allowance. The seam lines are crossed by other lines of stitching so there is no need to backstitch to stop the thread from unravelling.

In a repeat block quilt, if the same pair of pieces in each block need to be sewn together many times, the process can be speeded up by chaining (Diagram 19). Feed the next pair in as the last clears the needle without snipping the thread between them, so that a long chain of sewing forms. Snip the pairs apart, press them and stack them in order so that they can be chained to the next piece in the next step.

It is easier to sew two lots of cross seams together if the seams on the top layer face away from you and the seams on the bottom layer lie towards you as they pass through the sewing machine, so press accordingly. The bottom seams feed evenly over the feed dog and the top layer, the movement of which is slightly retarded as it moves under the presser foot, locks into the underlying seam line. This gives a precise intersection of seams.

PRESSING

After sewing each seam line, press the seam allowances. First press the seam allowances to one side on the back of the work, then

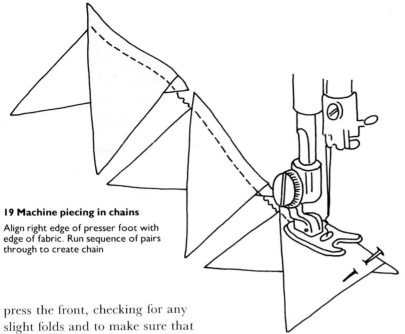

19 Machine piecing in chains
Align right edge of presser foot with edge of fabric. Run sequence of pairs through to create chain

press the front, checking for any slight folds and to make sure that all points are cleanly exposed. Accuracy in pressing is essential or all those carefully crossed seams may not show as clean intersections. Do not drag the iron over the work, but lift it and press it down from one area to another. Some fabrics may need a pressing cloth to prevent glazing.

There are several conflicting rules for pressing seam allowances, so decide what works best for a particular block. In general, press towards the darker fabric because the seams are less likely to show through on this side. In hand piecing, the cross seams are free and can be pressed either way. With machine pieced work the seams are caught into

20 Pressing

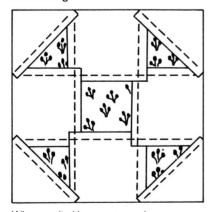

Where applicable, press towards darker fabrics

the next line of stitching so you will have less choice in the direction for ironing (Diagram 20).

The very fine points of a Mariner's Compass and Eight-Point Star should all be pressed in the same direction, say clockwise. If there is a point where many seams come together, it may be necessary to consider reducing the fabric bulk by snipping off the points and trimming the seam allowance.

Another thing to consider when ironing the seams is the quilting pattern. Whenever possible it is easier and more sightly to quilt through the minimum number of fabrics, so the seams should be pressed accordingly.

LOG CABIN

Log Cabin is a block category that is based on an isolated central square surrounded by strips of fabric called logs. Log Cabin reads as a block cut diagonally in half, with one half light and the other dark. The arrangement of these lights and darks, the

manipulation of the width of the log, colouring, and the placement of the centre in each block allow for an enormous variety of effects (see Diagrams 21a, b and c on page 74). The placement of lights and darks in Susan McIver's *Lollipop Lane* (see page 74) creates diagonal rows, and this arrangement is traditionally known as Straight Furrows.

The central square in a Log Cabin block was traditionally red to recall a fire burning in a hearth. The light side of the block symbolised not only the light coming from the fire, but the light of civilisation, while the dark area represented the shadows and the unknown. Sometimes, however, the central square was yellow, a colour chosen to signify the light in a window. These squares appeared to float in the background of strips if the strips were in muted colours. Stripes and checks were often used in the logs to introduce an unexpected effect, particularly if they were not cut precisely along the line of the fabric pattern.

Because Log Cabin usually has the central square surrounded by straight logs, it is often made up without drafting. Rather than cutting each log, the fabrics can be cut in strips of even width. They are trimmed to length after sewing. The central squares should be cut very accurately because any error tends to accumulate as each round of logs is added, but even this can be fixed by squaring off the finished block. While this might require chopping off part of the logs, the errors are not obvious when they are sewn to the other blocks.

This slightly haphazard approach adds charm to many quilts, and means that they can be whipped up without too much attention to precision.

Common settings for Log Cabin

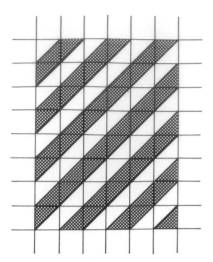

21a Straight Furrows

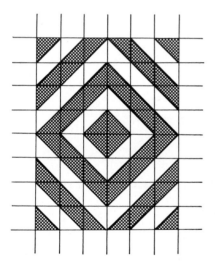

21b Barn Raising

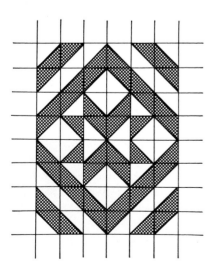

21c Log Cabin Star

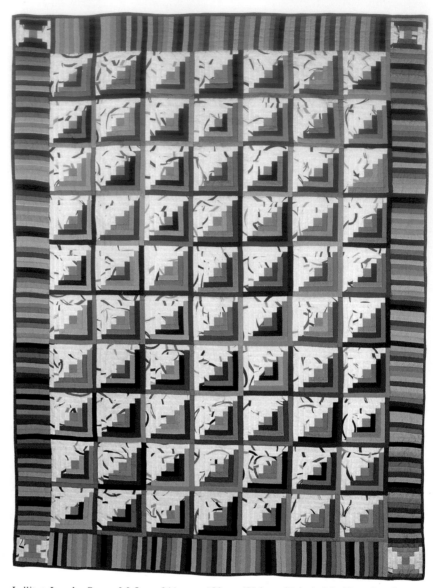

Lollipop Lane by Susan McIver. 241 cm x 180 cm (95 in. x 71 in.). Machine pieced. Hand quilted. Log Cabin

If, however, the quilt needs to be a specific size, or if a Log Cabin block needs to fit into an otherwise accurate sampler quilt, then the block should be drafted.

DRAFTING

Evenly divide the total quilt area to be covered into blocks to obtain the dimensions of an individual block. Next, decide on the size of the central square and the number of logs to be fitted around it. The square is usually twice the width of a log, and 10 to 12 logs

across a block is a good number.

Make a square block and draw the diagonals. If the central square is not to be once or twice the width of a log, draw this, measuring out from the centre. If the measurement of the central square is a multiple of the log width, count the number of log widths (including those across the central square) across the block and divide one side into this many equal units (see Drafting Blocks With Regular Grids, page 68). Construct the uprights through these points, drawing only be-

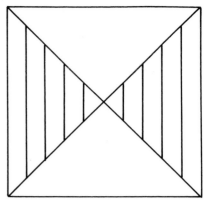

22a After drafting a block, draw in diagonals and then drop in perpendiculars

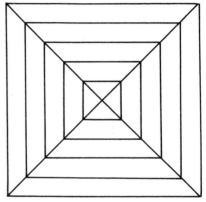

22b Construct horizontals to complete squares

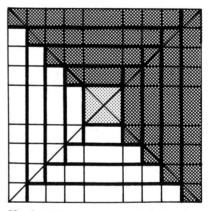

22c Carefully mark in logs in spiral around central square. Shade in dark side

Log Cabin Cover by Greg Somerville. 210 cm x 205 cm (82½ in. x 80½ in.). Hand pieced, appliquéd and quilted

Drafting Log Cabin

tween the diagonals (Diagram 22a).

If the central square is not a multiple of the log width, measure the distance between the edge of the central square and the size of the block. This is the distance that will be divided into log widths.

Having constructed the uprights, now use the same procedure to create the horizontals. Once all the points along the sides of the block have been connected to their opposite number, the construction lines will form squares (22b). Next draw in the logs (22c). The logs build out around the centre in a spiral. The first one is the same length as the square, so extend the lines down from the central square to complete the first log. The next one is the width of the first block plus the side of the

square. The third is the same. The fourth is the width of two logs plus the side of the square. The first round is now complete. Each round must start on the same side and in this manner the logs step out towards the edge of the block.

MARKING AND CUTTING

Depending on how accurate it needs to be, each log can be cut individually, or the fabric can be cut along the cross grain into log widths. Each strip should be the width of the log plus two seam allowances. The centre square should be cut precisely, with seam allowances added.

The selection of tones in the fabrics is vital. As mentioned earlier, half the block traditionally comprises lighter fabrics than the

other. But other effects can be produced: for instance, solids read more strongly than prints and if they are interspersed with prints a subpattern can form. Consider also how the outside ring of fabrics will relate to the adjacent blocks. If the same fabrics come together it can be overwhelming

Piecing order for Log Cabin

23a Sew strip to central square

23b Finger press open

23c Sew on second strip to adjacent side

23d Repeat with first strip of second pair

23e Complete the round

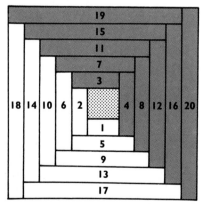

23f Finished block showing piecing order

and become the dominant feature of the quilt. Still, Greg Somerville uses this effect to great advantage in *Log Cabin Cover* (see page 75).

SEWING

Log Cabin lends itself to machine piecing. The log can be sewn directly around the centre alone or it can be sewn through to a foundation fabric for strength and accuracy. The foundation could be a layer of batting, in which case the sewing and quilting are done in one step.

The logs in the first pair of sides cover slightly less area in the finished quilt than the second pair, so decide which fabric, the light or dark, should be less important and use it first. The quilt will be lighter or darker as a result.

With the right sides together, carefully aligning the edges, sew the first strip to the central square (Diagram 23a). Sew from edge to edge, even if you are working by hand. Trim the log parallel to the edge of the square. Open out the log and finger press (23b). Repeat the first step, aligning the next log with the square plus the first log (23c). Change the tone of the fabric for the next two sides (23d). The first round is now complete (23e). Continue the process in the same direction, keeping lights to one side and darks to the other (23f).

Rather than completing each block individually, the assembly can be speeded up by chaining on the sewing machine. Take the first strip with its right side up and lay the central square onto it, matching right-hand edges. Run them through the sewing machine, stitching along this edge, and position the next square

so that it abuts the first. All the squares can be sewn to the strip one after the other (Diagram 24a). Cut apart and finger press open (24b). These new units (centre plus strip) can now be fed through the machine, face down on the next strip (24c). Repeat the process until the blocks are finished.

Arrange the finished blocks to create the desired pattern of lights and darks, then sew them together. Trim away seam allowances to reduce the bulk. If you are sewing by hand, backstitch for strength. Press the seam allowances apart to reduce the bulk.

The old Log Cabins were frequently finished with only a binding (and no borders), but this can be varied. Susan McIver made a border of the darker strips and filled in the corners with the Court House Steps pattern, a variation on Log Cabin.

QUILTING

Because of the thickness of the seam allowances, Log Cabin is often tied rather than quilted. When it *is* quilted, the line usually follows the seam line, on the side with the least amount of fabric thickness. Sometimes every row of logs is stitched along, sometimes every second or third. Another possibility is a spider web quilting pattern across each block, although this means that you have to quilt through the seam allowances. Thus, while there is less stitching, it is more difficult.

VARIATIONS ON LOG CABIN

COURT HOUSE STEPS

The drafting is similar to Log Cabin, only the order of sewing changes. Draft up the series of

**Machine sewing
Log Cabin**

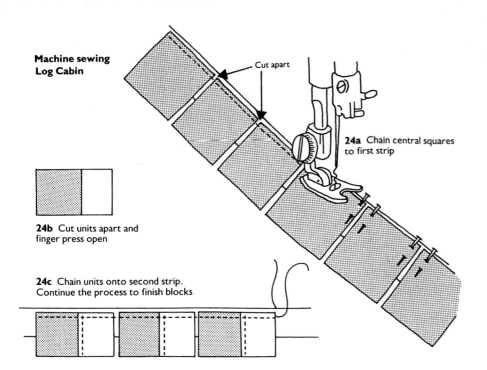

Cut apart

24a Chain central squares
to first strip

24b Cut units apart and
finger press open

24c Chain units onto second strip.
Continue the process to finish blocks

Piecing order for Court House Steps

25a Sew first strip to central square

25b Finger press open

25c Sew second strip to opposite side

squares, then the first log (as described in the basic Log Cabin technique), but the second log is placed above the square and measures the same length as the first (Diagrams 25a, b and c). The next pair of logs in the round are placed on either side of the square and so should measure the width of the square plus the width of two logs (25d, e and f).

The first pair of logs is sewn on opposite sides of the central square. The second pair of logs completes the new square. Succeeding rounds start on the sides with the shortest steps.

OFF-CENTRE LOG CABIN

In this variation the sewing sequence is the same as the traditional Log Cabin, but the square around which the logs build out is not centred in the block. Once it is located, draft as before, but one pair of logs will be much narrower than the other (Diagram 26).

The shading of light and dark takes on a rounded appearance, as in Pamela Tawton's *Moonriver* (see page 19).

26 Drafting Off-centre Log Cabin

The square is *not* centred and the two sets of logs are different widths

PINEAPPLE

Pineapple is a variation of Log Cabin that has logs not only on the horizontal and vertical but also on the diagonal. Hence rounds have eight logs rather than just four which helps to create a jagged edge rather than the stepped appearance of the others described.

Often these logs are sewn directly to the central square and the finished block size is not calculated in advance. It is, however, possible to draft this pattern precisely, which is what

25d Sew first strip of second pair to adjacent side

25e Complete the round

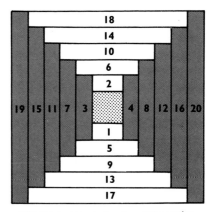

25f Finished block showing piecing order

we will do. This drafted plan indicates where the light and dark fabrics will fall, and the order of sewing.

Draft a square the size of the finished block and draw in the diagonals and quarter lines. Then draft the central square and surrounding series of squares as for regular Log Cabin. This gives the sewing lines for the logs on the horizontal and vertical. To create the sewing lines for those logs on the diagonal, a new series of squares on the point is drafted. Draw the first square on the point from diagonal to diagonal, passing through the corners of the central square (Diagram 27a).

Further squares on the point, only one log width apart, are now added around this (27b).

There are now two sets of overlapping squares, the overlap increasing towards the corners of the block. Carefully consider the construction lines of the block. Now strengthen the sewing lines for the Pineapple logs. Having decided on the arrangement of lights and darks, one set is always sewn on the horizontal and vertical lines, the other always on the diagonal. Each round of logs consists of two sets of four logs: one set light, the other set dark. The first set is sewn to the four sides of the central square, the

next set to the first square on the point. The next round of logs falls within the two sets of squares. The corners of the first set of squares are eliminated. The next round cuts off the corners of the square on the point. Continue to strengthen the design lines in rounds to distinguish them from the construction lines. Once you have finished, shade in the dark logs to make the pattern obvious.

Cut out a template of the central square first. Then cut strips the width of the logs, plus seam allowances, in the light and dark fabrics you have chosen. The logs will be trimmed to shape after sewing. Pineapple is easy to sew, but may at first appear confusing because the logs overlap to create jagged angles.

To assist in the placement of the logs, a backing square with diagonal and quarter lines marked on it is useful. Cut this square to the size of the finished

Drafting, Piecing and Sewing Pineapple

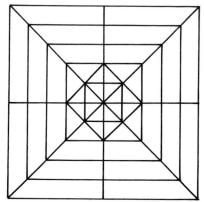

27a Draft a square. Mark in diagonals and quarter lines. Draft central square and rounds of logs as in Diagrams 22a–c. Draw first square on point passing through corner of central square, from diagonal to diagonal

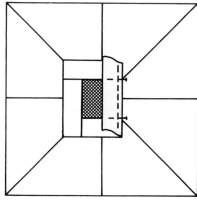

27c Cut out backing square (including seam allowances) and mark in diagonals and quarter lines. Make templates of central squares and long strips for logs. Cut out pieces in light and dark fabrics. Sew first round of light logs as for regular Log Cabin

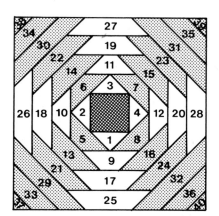

27e Continue to sew round until block is complete: light logs as for regular Log Cabin and dark logs around square set on point. Trim excess triangles of fabric

27b Construct further series of squares on point. Darken design lines, disregarding superfluous corners of squares

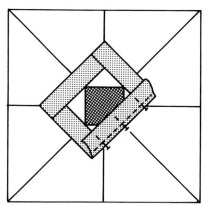

27d Sew round of dark logs, positioning pins on diagonals and quarter lines of backing fabric. Central pin passes through corner of central square

block, plus seam allowances. Place the central square in position on it, right side up and with its corners on the diagonal lines of the backing fabric.

The block can be sewn by hand or machine. For this example, light logs are sewn first. Sew the first light log to one edge of the square and trim to size, leaving a seam allowance. Finger press back and pin. Repeat for each light log in this round (27c). Take a dark strip, wrong side up, and place it on the diagonal. Pin through the sewing line at the corner of the square and the quarter lines. The pins will pass through the sewing line of the light log already sewn (27d). Trim the first round of logs on the diagonal to eliminate the corners of excess fabric. Finger press back and pin. Repeat for each log to complete the round. The next light round is pinned through its sewing line to the intersecting

sewing line of the dark log that underlies it. Also pin through the diagonal mark on the backing fabric. Sew, trim and press as before. Continue to sew rounds until the block is complete (27e).

There are more logs on the diagonal than on the straight if they are continued through to the corners. It is possible to fill in these corners with a large triangle of fabric rather than the last logs. Consider, however, the effect of four of these triangles abutting when blocks are sewn together.

When the blocks are complete, turn to the back and trim the backing fabric to the stitching lines to eliminate bulk when the blocks are sewn together. Any minor inaccuracies can be hidden by trimming the blocks to size. Backstitch when sewing the blocks together by hand. So many layers are being sewn through that a running stitch would not be firm enough.

CURVED SEAMS

Piecing is usually associated with sewing straight lines and appliqué with curved seam lines, but curved seams are also possible in piecing. Curved lines reduce the number of seams because they can eliminate corners and extra seam lines as well as extending the range of design possibilities. They are handy in pictorial quilts.

Drunkard's Path is a category of four-patch patterns that has only two curved templates that fit together to make a square. (Remember that, although I have centred my discussion about curved seams on Drunkard's Path, many other designs are possible once the techniques have been mastered.)

The illustrations on page 163 show several arrangements that result from rotating the unit. Bronwen Schwarze's *Yellow*

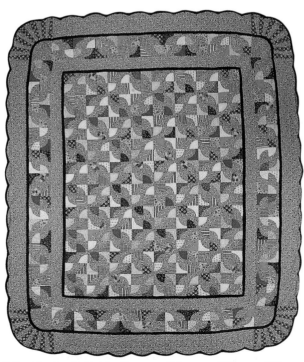

Yellow Drunkard's Path by Bronwen Schwarze. 280 cm x 240 cm (110 in. x 94½ in.). Hand and machine pieced. Hand quilted. Drunkard's Path

Appletree by Christa Roksandic. 195 cm x 150 cm (77 in. x 59 in.). Machine pieced curved seams. Hand quilted. Drunkard's Path variations

Drunkard's Path (see page 79) is one such arrangement for a whole quilt.

Variation to the design can be introduced by changing the placement of fabrics. When she first learnt patchwork, Christa Roksandic was entranced by the possibilities of the curved seam and, one week, instead of making a block, she whipped up *Appletree* (see page 79). In this quilt she used the same unit as Drunkard's Path, with the inclusion of some squares, but by rotating the block and planning the colour, came up with her own original design, a picture quilt rather than the more usual geometric design. The flexibility of curved seams continues to inspire her. Now, rather than working within a regular grid, she drafts up her pattern, subdivides it into component blocks of sizes that accommodate the design, and pieces it.

Fiona Gavens's *The Hollow Tree* (see page 27) is one of a series of quilts using tight curved seams and a few repeated templates. In *Cockies Naive* Jennifer Lewis pieced the background of each block in curved strips, the templates for which were drawn freehand. The blocks are all the same design, but read quite differently because of the placement of colour and because they have been rotated. The cockies were then appliquéd over the top of the blocks.

DRAFTING

The many design possibilities which curved piecing allows require different approaches that are not easily categorised. This being the case, here are a few principles which are useful to follow.

Old quilts were obviously made without the benefit of compasses,

Cockies Naive by Jennifer Lewis. 117 cm x 104 cm (46 in. x 41 in.). Hand pieced, embroidered, appliquéd and quilted

so everyday household utensils like plates and teacups were traced around to create circles. To describe a large circle, a thumbtack in a piece of string would secure it to the centre point, and a pencil tied in the string at the appropriate distance would give a circle of any size.

These days, however, precision is believed to be important, so compasses are used. To obtain the arc within the smallest unit of a Drunkard's Path, place the compass point on a corner of the unit square (point 0) and extend it to describe an arc that intersects two sides of the square (Diagram 28a). The arc should be at least halfway up each side, but should not intersect the corners of the square.

If you will be piecing by machine, the compass can be extended and closed by 5 mm ($\frac{1}{4}$ in.) to draw the cutting lines (28b). For hand sewing mark in the sewing line only. It needs to be absolutely precise. You can judge the width of the seam allowances with your eye as you cut (28c).

For some patterns the line obtained using a compass may be *too* curved. To flatten the curve, draw a diagonal line connecting opposite corners of the square and extend it beyond the square. Move the compass point up and down the line and try several compass widths, describing arcs until you find a satisfactory curve.

For a freehand design that will be pieced on the machine, draft up the whole design for each

Drafting curved seams

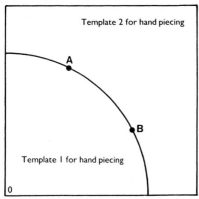

28a Draft a block and describe an arc with compass on point 0. Mark pinning points A and B

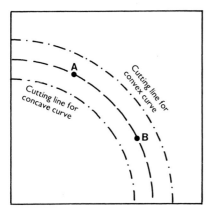

28b Add seam allowances to give templates for machine piecing

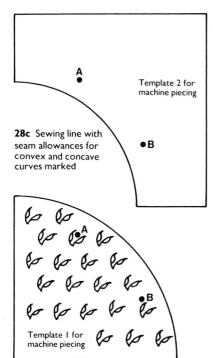

28c Sewing line with seam allowances for convex and concave curves marked

template. Adding the seam allowance is done by a different method in this case: use a compass opened to the width of the seam allowance and, tracing the point along the line and keeping the pencil lead at right angles to it, draw the cutting line. The template can then be cut from this new shape. As the template for the adjacent shape has its cutting line within the first shape, be careful not to become confused about which line belongs to which shape.

Piecing a concave curve to a convex one is not as easy as piecing two straight seams. Make the task simpler by marking pinning points across the seam lines onto adjacent patches. These points are transferred from the templates to the fabric to indicate where to pin.

SEWING AND PRESSING

When you are pinning curved lines together it may be necessary to clip into the seam allowance of the concave side to make it lie flat. Hand sewing curved seams is a little harder than sewing straight lines because the seam lines need to be checked with each needleful of stitches to ensure that they are matched. Initially it is easier to use a lot of pins (Diagram 29). However, as you become practised in sewing curved seams by machine you will eventually need fewer pins. Sewing from pin to pin on the machine can result in a series of straight lines. With practice you can use the point of a seam ripper on the seam line to hold the lines together until they pass under the needle. Curved seams can be pressed to either side (Diagram 30).

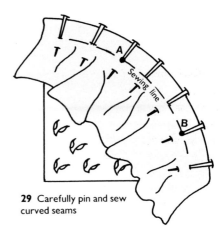

29 Carefully pin and sew curved seams

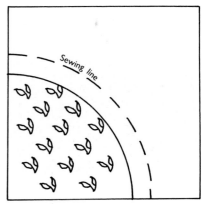

30 Press seam allowances to one side

QUILTING

The seam line is often followed for quilting, emphasising the curved pieces. Christa Roksandic's *Pools of Peace* (see page 83) uses the quilting in this manner, and the individual pieces seem stuffed. The shiny fabrics catch the light.

PIECED MEDALLION QUILTS

A medallion quilt has a central feature block surrounded by several borders. Frequently, the borders themselves are pieced. There is often a radiating pattern, with elements (like shapes or colour) of one part repeated

Miniature Medallion Quilt by Trudy Brodie. 40 cm x 34 cm (15½ in. x 13½ in.). Hand pieced and quilted

that the sides can be longer than the top and bottom. Because you know how to divide up a side evenly, regardless of its length, you can give an old block a new look by elongating it.

Drafting, sewing and quilting of medallion quilts are common to other pieced quilts, so follow the instructions for those.

PIECED PICTURES

A category of quilts that can be planned ahead, but which does not rely on a grid system for drafting, is the pieced picture. More or less realistic, depending on the quiltmaker, the image represented is often a landscape. Because these landscapes may not show up well on a bed with its drops, the quilts are usually wall pieces, and have a horizontal format. The wall quilt is not subjected to washing so a wide range of fabrics can be used. For instance, net can be sewn over areas to soften the focus or to suggest distance.

The picture is often reduced to a cartoon — a full-scale drawing of the design with individual pattern pieces. It is often useful to create the design on a wide sheet of plastic using a water-soluble felt-tip pen. This way corrections can be made easily. Alternatively, produce a small version of the design initially, then, if you have access to an overhead projector or a photocopier that enlarges, you won't have to resort to doing the enlargement by hand on a grid (see page 93).

To assist piecing, the overall design is usually broken up into construction units that may not be apparent when the top is complete. These blocks can be squares, rectangles, triangles or

elsewhere to unify the whole. The quilt can be carefully planned so that all the fabrics coordinate and the patterns in the pieced borders turn the corners in a regular manner, or they can be composed of scraps sewn together without regard to accuracy or repetition.

Trudy Brodie's *Miniature Medallion Quilt* is a fine example of good use of fabric. Elements in the fabric design are positioned to add to the design of the piecing. The colours and part of the design of the central block are repeated in the corners of two borders, and the darkest fabric is repeated as the ground of several blocks. The diamond-on-square set alternates, with the scale increasing in size as it moves out from the centre.

The construction of a medallion quilt does not need separate instructions. Just follow the directions for pieced blocks and

borders. What is important is the scale of one border to the next; making the whole work is a matter of balance and unity.

Most beds require rectangular quilts, while most blocks are squares, so just adding borders the same width all the way around is not enough. Plan some way to elongate the quilt top into a rectangle. One possible arrangement is shown in Diagram 31. The four squares in the centre could incorporate a particular block and the same block could be repeated in a surrounding border. By having one and a half blocks on the top and bottom, and only one block on the sides, the quilt top turns into a rectangle.

Another design solution is to use a rectangular block in the centre instead of the traditional square. Now that you know how to draft a block you will realise

31 An arrangement for a medallion quilt

Border with isolated
corner squares

Border with isolated
square corners

Border with mitred corners

Border one block wide

Border 1½ blocks wide

Binding

Glenquarry by Robyn Cooper. 164 cm x 134 cm (64½ in. x 53 in.). Machine pieced. Hand appliquéd. Machine quilted

32 Christa Roksandic's working drawing for *Pools of Peace* — a pieced picture

Pools of Peace by Christa Roksandic. 195 cm x 190 cm (77 in. x 75 in.). Machine pieced. Hand quilted

any shape that is easily sewn to the next unit.

Trudy Billingsley's work has already been mentioned, and Christa Roksandic uses the same approach, but often includes curved lines in her design. Compare, for example, the diagram of her *Pools of Peace* with the photograph of the finished quilt. Robyn Cooper's *Glenquarry* uses strip pieced units and includes chequerboard houses with stripped roofs to represent the landscape around Glenquarry. The house blocks were, in fact, left over from another quilt, a great example of recycling.

The individual pattern pieces can be decided first and the fabric cut to the templates, or the fabrics can dictate shapes and combinations, with the units formed trimmed to size so that they can be sewn to others. A full-size drawing or cartoon is useful for orchestrating the overall design. Do not cut this up, but trace off templates and number them according to the numbering on the cartoon so that you will know where to place them. Mark in the long grain on the template, because even if the fabric is not cut with reference to it, it will help position the piece in the unit.

Many of the quick cutting and sewing techniques are not applicable to pieced pictures because the pieces in the units are likely to vary from one to another. The work can be hand or machine pieced. The order of sewing should build up the pieces into rows or blocks that sew onto others, but without having to sew into inset corners. The sewing technique is the same as for pieced blocks. Quilting is likely to be independent of seam lines, as the pieces are put together to create the overall picture rather than as individual elements to be isolated by the quilting line. More appropriate is a design encompassing the whole quilt top, complementing the picture.

STRIP PIECING

Whereas most pieced quilts are drafted, the templates made and the fabric then cut into these patterns, strip quilts allow much more freedom. Usually the strips have parallel sides, while the width varies from one strip to another. The width can depend on the strength of the colour or the image required. The strip need not incorporate the same fabric along its length. In *Terra Australis* (see page 34) I sometimes ran out of fabrics, so I would substitute another fabric in a similar colour and tone, although the print would be very different. If joining fabrics, make a feature of it so it does not look as if you only did it because you ran out of material. In *Japanese*

Mischa's Quilt by Robyn Cooper. 210 cm x 120 cm (82½ in. x 47 in.). Machine pieced and quilted

Hillside (see page 17), Prue Socha deliberately changed fabrics to create the picture she desired.

The colours and prints of the fabrics are what give this technique its interest. To control

this, Marli Popple dyed her own fabrics for *Broulee* (see page 38). For *Mischa's Quilt*, Robyn Cooper stripped together fabrics in gradations from light to dark. Having created yardage, she cut the stripped fabric into triangles and recombined these in rows on the diagonal. Thus a very straightforward design can be given complexity and surprise effects by the use of stripped fabric. The border of *Mischa's Quilt* is also stripped and integrated into the overall pattern, but by keeping the angle of cuts consistent around the whole quilt, while the internal rows alternate in direction, the border remains separate.

CUTTING

A template is not necessary for cutting out the strips, and it would be a nuisance to cut individual ones if all the strips were different widths. This is a case where the gridded perspex ruler, rotary cutter and cutting board are wonderful. Because cutting boards are usually only as wide as *half* a normal width of fabric, fold the fabric in half lengthwise, measure the required width with the ruler and cut. Even after sewing, if the effect is not right, a strip can be cut along its length and narrowed, or more added. No marking is necessary and the lines on the grid will ensure that the cutting lines are parallel.

If you do not have a gridded ruler, rip across the fabric to find the cross grain. Fold in half lengthwise, matching the edges. The cross grain and the long grain should be at right angles. If they are not quite perpendicular, you could press them true; otherwise do not fold the fabric. Measure from the ripped end along each long grain edge to mark the strip widths and cut along the new lines. If using scissors, mark this line. The strips need not be parallel: they can be random widths, narrow one end and wider on the other.

Sunburst by Dianne Finnegan. 39 cm x 29 cm (15 ½ in. x 11 ½ in.). Machine pieced and quilted

Instead of cutting you can rip the fabric on the cross grain. The strips will automatically be an even width because all cross grains are parallel to one another. Some fabrics fray more than others, so consider the edge to be halfway in from the frayed threads and allow for this when ripping and sewing.

SEWING

Strip piecing fabric is very fast, because there are no intersecting seams to consider, just straight lines of sewing. It is usually done on the machine — there is no advantage to be gained by hand sewing. Machine work is essential if the strips are to be recut after being sewn together because machine sewing locks crossed lines of stitching together. Hand sewn lines would unravel.

Once the strips are sewn together, the new yardage can be trimmed to the required size. Stripped fabric can be used as the backing fabric for an appliqué design, or be cut into shapes that are then sewn together in another pattern as in *Mischa's Quilt*.

If the grain line is inconsistent, the strips can be sewn together on a backing fabric, giving the whole stability and strength.

My miniature *Sunburst* is radial (see page 85). Although the angles appear to be random, I had drafted on paper a square larger than the finished size, ruled into quarters, and with the diagonals marked. Every few strips I would lay the sewing on the square and work out how much I would need to compensate in order to keep the strips radiating in roughly a circular manner. The last strip had to be taken in precisely to complete the circle so that it lay flat, then the centre was inserted.

PRESSING

Always press the seam allowances of a set of strips in the same direction, especially if they are being recut.

QUILTING

The strips can be quilted along the seam lines in the ditch as in *Sunburst* (see page 85), or another pattern can be imposed on the stripping. This design can be a whole quilt design, perhaps in sweeping concentric curves, or it could form in response to the fabrics. Bands of colours were quilted in designs in the fabric to suggest weathering patterns in rock in *Terra Australis* (see page 34).

SEMINOLE

With the invention of the sewing machine, new techniques that were not possible with hand piecing were developed. The Seminole Indians developed a way of creating bands of patterns without cutting out individual pieces. Although apparently intricate, the construction is

Semi-blue by Anne Moten. 180 cm x 150 cm (71 in. x 59 in.). Machine pieced. Hand quilted. Seminole

simple. Strips of fabric are joined into rows or bands, then the whole band is cut into narrow sets which are realigned before being sewn again to form new patterns. Seminole strips cannot be hand sewn because the lines of sewing are cut and hand sewing would unravel. Ann Moten's seminole quilt, *Semi-Blue*, shows the variety of patterns that can be produced with this technique.

MARKING, CUTTING AND SEWING

As with other forms of strip piecing, rotary cutters and gridded perspex rulers are helpful. They eliminate the need to mark the fabric because the strip width can be measured on the ruler, which then acts as a guide for the rotary cutter. All

seam allowances are 5 mm ($\frac{1}{4}$ in.), which should be the distance between the needle and the edge of the presser foot on the sewing machine. The edge of the fabric is aligned with the edge of the presser foot so that the needle must sew exactly the correct width for the seam allowance.

Chain sewing (see Diagram 19 on page 73) is another time saver. When sewing a series of repeat units, feed each one in as the last passes out from under the needle without snipping the thread. The chain of strips can be snipped apart when the units are pressed.

ROWS OF SEMINOLE

Different patterns result from varying the angle at which bands of fabric are cut. The first group of patterns are made by cutting at right angles to the stitching through the bands of strips.

A set with several strips cut on the perpendicular (Diagram 33a), then offset by one row (33b), will give a pattern of squares on their point with a row of triangles above and below. A serrated edge develops from offsetting and often such bands are trimmed and enclosed in edging strips (33c).

Cutting the band on an angle produces a different effect (see Diagram 34a on page 88). By varying the angle of the cut and also the angle at which the segments are joined variations will also result (34b). The points in seminole may meet accurately, or may be arranged to overlap slightly, reducing the need for accuracy. By cutting half of the segments at one angle and the other as a mirror reverse (see Diagram 35a on page 88) it is possible to make a herringbone (35b). And by sewing bands onto patterns already made, then cutting again, offsetting and resewing, even more complex patterns develop.

Flipping every other segment can give a chequerboard effect, and insertions increase the complexity as shown in Diagram 36a on page 88. This pattern could be a block pattern (36b).

BLOCK PATTERNS

When many simple block patterns are analysed it becomes apparent that elements of them can be assembled using seminole. The red and yellow nine-patches in my *Red Cross* (see page 89) were very quickly sewn using seminole. In fact the quilt was designed to achieve maximum effect in the minimum time, and only took three days to make. Two lots of strips were sewn, one red, yellow, red, and the other yellow, red, yellow. Because the Nine Patch

Seminole (Offsetting squares with perpendicular cuts)

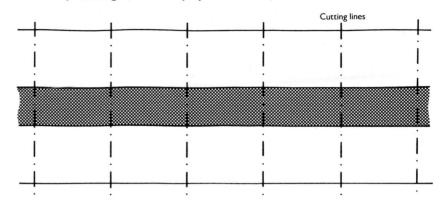

33a Sew three strips together, then mark perpendicular cutting lines. Cut apart

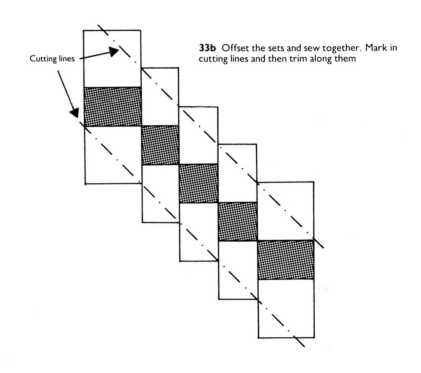

33b Offset the sets and sew together. Mark in cutting lines and then trim along them

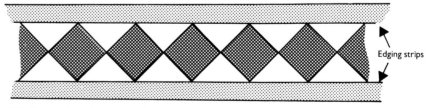

33c Sew edging strip onto band

Seminole (With diagonal cuts)

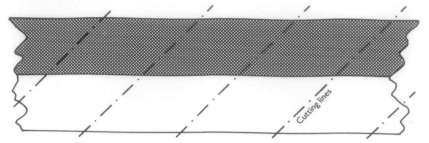

34a Sew strips together and mark cutting lines on an angle. Cut apart

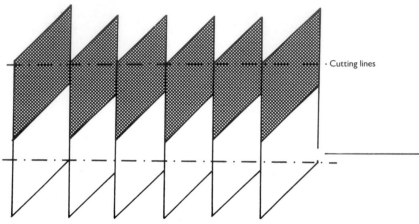

Cutting lines

34b Offset and sew the sets together. Mark in cutting lines and trim along them

Seminole (With diagonal cuts and mirror imaging)

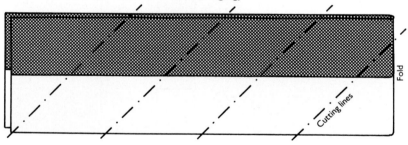

Fold

Cutting lines

35a Sew strips together, then fold set in half, matching seams. Mark cutting lines at an angle and cut apart

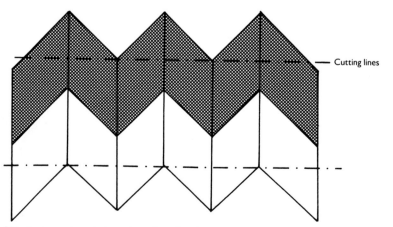

Cutting lines

35b Arrange mirror image pairs and sew into herringbone arrangement. Mark in cutting lines and trim along them

Seminole (With insertion and reversing strips)

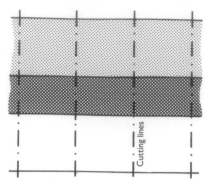

Cutting lines

36a Sew strips into sets, then mark cutting lines. Cut apart

Insertion

| Set | Insertion | Flipped set |

36b Sew in this order: one set, insertion, then one set flipped

had two rows of the first and one of the second, twice as many of the first band were sewn. The bands were sewn, cut into sets and then the sets were combined into the finished block.

Sometimes the block pattern may comprise more than one seminole unit that can be mass produced, then sewn together into the block at the end.

NON-TRADITIONAL SEMINOLE

While I was making *Terra Australis* (see page 34), I had difficulty with the transition from one group of strips to another. No fabric I had would link the colours of the two groups, and when I tried a band of solid

Red Cross by Dianne Finnegan. 182 cm x 182 cm (71½ in. x 71½ in.). Machine pieced and quilted. Nine patch

fabrics they looked very static. In the end, because the quilt represented rock strata, I decided to cut up the band of strips into irregular segments, offset them, turn the occasional one upside down, insert a couple of hot pink intrusions and reassemble. The whole was supposed to represent a faulted geological zone, and, more importantly, link the two sets of strips.

In *Implicate Order No. 4* (see page 24), Greg Somerville built up the top by cutting a range of fabrics, inserting a new fabric, then cutting it all up again and inserting again. This particular quilt goes far beyond the realms of traditional seminole and the method of building it up is subservient to the overall impact. Nevertheless, as Greg says, he is using simple, traditional techniques. "There is nothing

new in my work, it is just how I put it together. The techniques are basic — it is just sewing strips."

EIGHT-POINT STAR AND VARIATIONS

The Eight-Point Star is a favourite pattern and Adèle Outteridge's *Miniature Star* (see page 90) is a fine example. It may be used in a block or as one star extended over an entire quilt. The latter lends itself to a seminole method of construction because the strips can be joined, cut on an angle, off set and resewn to form rows of diamonds in each star point.

DRAFTING

The Eight-Point Star is based on an octagon, and drafting it does not rely on the grids we have developed previously. Drafting for a block is very different from drafting for a whole quilt.

THE BLOCK

First construct a square of the required size, then mark into quarters and draw in the diagonals (see Diagram 37a on page 90). With your compass point on 0, the intersection of all the lines, describe a small circle with a diameter of about 2 cm (1 in.). Bisect the segments by placing the compass point on the intersection of all the lines and the circle, and describe arcs. The intersection of these arcs equally divides the space between each pair of lines (37b). Draw lines connecting opposite intersections, passing through the centre and extending to the square. Clearly label each new point where a line intersects the square A, B, C, etc (37c).

Starting from point A, count around three of these points to D and join AD. Repeat from B to construct line BE. Continue for each labelled point, joining CF, DG, EH, FA, GB and HC. All the construction lines for the Eight-Point Star are now in place (37d). The diamonds are parallelograms with equal sides and angles of 60° and 120°.

The diamonds may look too large, but they can be subdivided. One option is to bisect them lengthwise. If the two halves are alternately coloured light and dark, a three-dimensional folded fan effect is created. However, this also results in 16 points coming together in the centre, which can be daunting to sew.

Another option is to subdivide

Drafting an Eight-Point Star

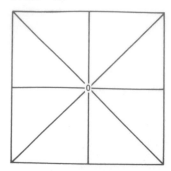

37a Draft a block. Draw in diagonals and quarter lines

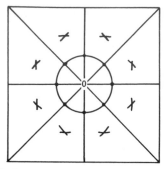

37b Describe circle at centre point 0. Position compass on each intersection of lines and circle in turn and describe arcs to bisect segments

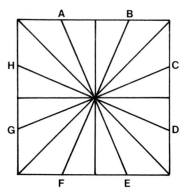

37c Connect opposite intersections of arcs and extend lines through to sides of block. Label these new intersections A to H

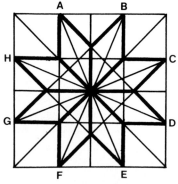

37d Join AD, BE, CF, DG, EH, FA, GB and HC. Then darken the lines forming points of star

Miniature Star by Adèle Outteridge. 46 cm x 46 cm (18 in. x 18 in.). Machine pieced. Hand quilted

each point of the diamond into smaller diamonds — two, three or more across depending on the size of the block. This is a usual technique to add interest in larger blocks. To bisect a side follow the instructions for dividing a line into equal parts on page 69.

THE WHOLE QUILT

If a large star quilt is to be machine sewn, the individual diamonds that make up each point are never handled separately.

MARKING, CUTTING AND SEWING

HAND PIECING

To reduce the likelihood of stretching ensure that two of the opposite sides of the diamond are on the grain line, because then only two edges will be on the bias.

If a stripe or some feature in the fabric is to be highlighted, however, this rule may not apply. Mark and cut shapes as for general hand piecing.

As with all piecing, the aim is to sew pieces into rows then into units. In this case the units are the eight points of the star. The star points are pieced together if they are made up of more than one piece, then pairs of the points are sewn together, and then the halves. At each stage press in a uniform direction so that later on the quilting will be consistent. Because the eye is drawn to the centre, care needs to be taken to ensure that the seam lines of the two halves line up perfectly: if the points do not meet the workmanship will seem poor. Therefore, match and pin each seam line intersection to ensure a good result. Press all the points in a clockwise direction, then trim the points at the centre to eliminate bulk in the seam allowances.

Another pitfall to avoid is excess fabric in the middle. When the pencil line is traced around a template onto the fabric, the size of each shape is increased minimally. This error will accumulate, which means that when the eight points are eventually joined, the centre of the star may not lie flat or there may be a hole there. To prevent this happening, sew just inside the seam line for the last few centimetres towards the centre.

At the centre, end the sewing line of each pair of seams in exactly the same hole, and backstitch on either side of the crossed seams when joining the halves.

The triangles and squares of background material are sewn in last; the inset corners cannot be avoided. See the general instructions on page 72 for these.

MACHINE PIECING

For a star with many diamonds in each point, seminole construction is the quickest method. Rather than handling individual pieces, strips of fabric are sewn together (Diagram 38a). They are then cut on a 45° angle, offset and resewn. The second row is offset by one strip of fabric, so one piece is unpicked from the top and sewn to the bottom, two from the next row and so on (38b). Sew these strips together in sequence, matching seam lines (38c). The bias edges need careful handling: only ever hold the pieces in the centre, never on the edge. Sew pairs of star points together; then sew quarters of the star together, then halves. As with hand piecing, the centrepoint needs special attention. It may be safer to sew from the centre out to the

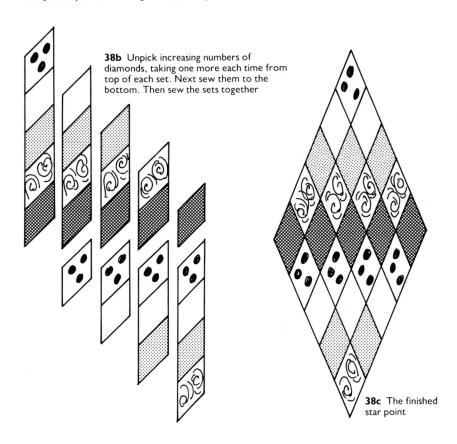

Seminole assembly of Eight-Point Star

Cutting lines at 45° to strip

38a Join strips, mark cutting lines and cut apart

38b Unpick increasing numbers of diamonds, taking one more each time from top of each set. Next sew them to the bottom. Then sew the sets together

38c The finished star point

edges. Sew background squares and triangles to the star when it is complete. These squares and triangles are inset corners (see page 72) when pieced between the points of the star. At each inset corner, make sure that the needle is down in the exact intersection of the seam lines, then lift the presser foot and rotate the fabrics until they are lined up parallel to the edge of the presser foot. With the point of the seam ripper, rotate the underlying fabric so that it will be flat for the

next line of sewing. Lower the presser foot. Sew out from the corner to the edge, completing the inset corner.

PRESSING

Press at each stage so that the seam allowances all lie in the same direction — for example, clockwise around the centre. Disregard the tone of the fabric.

QUILTING

Each diamond can be quilted, or bands of colour can be quilted around the star. The large triangles and squares in the background fabric offer scope for an interesting design, but make the quilting patterns in each relate. Do not use a grid that competes with the lines of piecing.

APPLIQUÉ

Appliqué lends itself to a more naturalistic, less geometric style than piecing. Instead of shapes being joined together to create yardage, in appliqué the shapes are sewn onto a background fabric.

Appliqué quilts are often pictorial, representing landscape elements. Because the elements are more flexible they can be freely drawn and arranged, allowing an enormous variation in style. Jocelyn Campbell's quiet, semi-realistic *Turtles at the Waterhole* contrasts with Denise Vanderlught's strongly coloured quilt (see page 15) that are direct representations of the natural environment in Queensland, while Marjorie Coleman's series of quilts depicting "dullflowers" celebrate the beauty of Australian flora (see page 13). Helen Macartney's *Water and Air* is a semi-realistic image; the waves are pieced and the birds are appliquéd to this background.

Still, the elements *can* be more regularly arranged into a pattern, or, alternatively, the shapes can be symmetrical, falling about one or more axes. Jeanette Parson's quilt of stylised flowers, *1000 Hours* (see page 94), is an example of such symmetrical patterns.

Water and Air by Helen Macartney. 128 cm x 122 cm (50½ in. x 48 in.). Machine appliquéd and pieced. Hand quilted

DESIGN

FREE FORM

Compose a scene, or adapt a photograph or something you have seen, then simplify the picture by eliminating any unnecessary elements and reducing acute angles which are harder to sew. If the picture is drawn onto grid paper it will be easier to scale to the finished size ready to make templates (Diagram 39a).

Grid up a piece of paper of the finished size, and enlarge the image from the original drawing to this size by reproducing the lines in each square (39b). The task will be made easier by marking the points where design lines cross the grid lines and then joining these points to complete

Turtles at the Waterhole (detail) by Jocelyn Campbell. 283 cm x 232 cm (111½ in. x 91½ in.). Thread painted. Hand appliquéd and quilted

Changing scale

39a (above) Draw a grid over the selected picture

39b (right) Draw a grid to required size. Mark in the intersection of image and grid lines from the original, then transfer the design lines

the picture. Alternatively, you can use an overhead projector or an enlargement photocopier to blow up the size of a pattern.

Do not cut out the master pattern, but overlay it with transparent template plastic and trace off the shapes. It is amazingly simple to confuse the shapes later on, or perhaps to flip them inadvertently, thus reversing the image, so number the shapes on the master pattern and on the corresponding templates for easy reference.

SYMMETRICAL DESIGNS

Patterns based on folded paper that has been cut into shapes and then opened out to reveal a symmetrical design have been developed independently in different parts of the world. For example, in Japan the style is know as Kirigami; in China, Hua Yang; in Poland, Wycinanki; and in Germany it is known as Scherenschnite. Appliqué based on folding was transported from Germany to America where it formed the basis for many designs. Smaller shapes in different coloured fabric could be appliquéd over the folded design

which was then laid on a background fabric. Colours were traditionally red, green, and a touch of yellow on a white or cream background. An American example of the technique is the Baltimore Bride Album quilts.

Sometimes called the Snowflake Method of creating symmetrical appliqué patterns, it was also developed into a local style called Hawaiian Appliqué (see page 98). The pattern is cut directly into the folded layers of fabric. When the fabric is unfolded, the mirror image pattern is revealed. There are a myriad patterns possible — as many kinds as there are different snowflakes, hence the name.

Most symmetrical appliqué is simple, but, to be on the safe side, confine your initial efforts to paper until an acceptable pattern is developed and refined before transferring it to the folded fabric.

CIRCULAR DESIGNS

Many appliqué designs are arranged around a circle: Jeanette Parsons's *1000 Hours* shows how the thin stems and vines trace the circle with the flowers positioned around it. The flowers can be evenly placed as here, or arranged in clumps (see the appliqué wreath in *Carly's Quilt* [see page 65] by Susan McIver).

MEDALLIONS

A medallion quilt format, in which a central feature is surrounded by borders, is a common layout for appliqué quilts. Elva Hine's *Floral Heirloom* is a stunning example of this approach. In this quilt, the central diamond of appliquéd flowers appears symmetrical, but on closer inspection you can see that the elements are specially

1000 Hours by Jeanette Parsons.
260 cm x 193 cm (102½ in. x 76 in.).
Hand appliquéd and quilted

Floral Heirloom by Elva Hine. 230 cm x 230 cm (90½ in. x 90½ in.). Hand overdyed prints and marbled fabrics. Hand appliquéd, pieced and quilted. Some stipple quilting

The Flower Press by Val Moore.
162 cm x 106 cm (64 in. x 41½ in.).
Machine appliquéd. Hand quilted.
Broderie Perse quilt arranging floral
prints. Prairie Point edging

balanced to give this effect.
Acknowledging the organic
nature of the subject, some of the
flowers stray over a border. The
edging is a strong pieced border,
but the soft colours prevent it
from being overwhelming. The
hand-dyed fabrics and use of
batiks give this quilt an obviously
Australian reference, even though
the flowers and birds are

reminiscent of a Baltimore Bride
Album quilt.

BRODERIE PERSE

When the highly prized chintzes
were scarce and expensive in early
America, quiltmakers cut out
precious motifs from the printed
fabric and spread them out to
make up a new design on a
background fabric. Whereas
appliqué is often confined to
solids, and the picture composed
of shapes that build up images, in
Broderie Perse the images are
already printed on the fabric.
Flowers were the most common
theme and Val Moore's *The
Flower Press* is an example of this.

No templates are needed
because the printed motifs
provide the shape. In appliqué
the thread is chosen to match the
top fabric, but in Broderie Perse

the colour of the fabric can vary
around the shape, so if you cannot
be bothered changing the thread
constantly, the stitching will be
more or less visible. To overcome
this, the shapes are often cut out
including a thin edge of the
background fabric, and the thread
can be chosen to match this.

HAND APPLIQUÉ

MARKING AND CUTTING

Cut out the backing fabric so that
it is the required size plus seam
allowances.

Overlay the sheet of template
plastic on the master plan,
transferring the outline, long
grain and shape number. Cut out
the template and position it on the
right side of the appropriate
fabric, aligning long grains. Trace

around the shape.

Unlike piecing, the shape is transferred to the right side of the fabric with the sewing line clearly visible, requiring you to turn back and baste the seam allowance. The long grain of the appliqué shapes should run up and down like the background fabric. (Feature fabrics are the exception to this rule. Val Moore cut out tiny flowers and other motifs and positioned them to create a pretty design in her quilt, *The Flower Press*. This technique, called Broderie Perse, is described above. In such cases the design overrides the rule of matching long grains.)

Cut the shape 5 mm ($\frac{1}{4}$ in.) larger than the finished size. Using the point of the scissors, clip the seam allowance at right angles to the sewing line along any curves to make it easier to fold over the seam allowance. For convex curves, cut out small wedges to reduce bulk in the seam allowance (Diagram 40a); for concave curves, snip so that the seam allowance can be turned back (40b). Trim any points and carefully snip almost to the seam line in the inner points or valleys to allow the seam to be turned under (40c).

Examine the master plan and decide which shapes will lie under others. These hidden edges do not need to be basted. By not basting them, additional bulk in the seams is avoided, and you eliminate the possibility of edges not quite meeting. Remember that convex curves are easier to

Clipping curves for basting

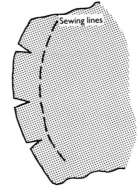

40a Convex curves should be notched in the seam allowance

40b Concave curves should be snipped in the seam allowance

sew than concave ones, so place them on top if possible.

Baste all the other seam allowances, using the marked seam lines as fold guides. Because pure cotton retains a crease, it is easily finger pressed and basted, and so is ideal for this technique. Polyester is specifically designed to withstand creasing so any blend with a high proportion of polyester will be far more difficult to hand appliqué.

Baste with the right side towards you, beginning and ending with a knot on the right side. To make turning easier, you can score the seam line with a blunt point, such as an orange stick or metal nail file, creating a crease that helps folding. To create a point, snip off the excess

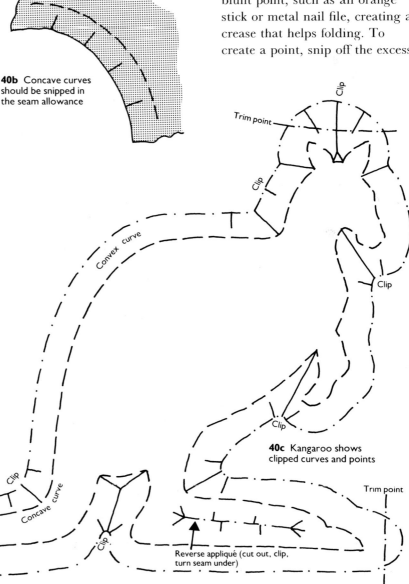

40c Kangaroo shows clipped curves and points

Reverse appliqué (cut out, clip, turn seam under)

Trim point

Cutting line

Basting a point

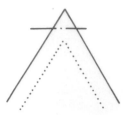

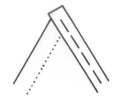

41a Trim excess seam allowance from point

41b Turn and baste first side

41c Fold point down

41d Baste second side

seam allowance (Diagram 41a), then baste the first side (41b). Turn down the seam allowance at right angles to the point (41c), then fold over the seam allowance on the next edge and baste (41d).

Small circles are difficult to turn evenly, so cut out a cardboard template and place it in position on the wrong side of the fabric. Then run a basting thread around the seam allowance and draw it up over the template. Press the circle with an iron, then remove the basting thread and template, and a perfect circle will be left. Other difficult shapes with sharp curves may also become easier to handle if you use an extra cardboard

template as a pressing template in the same manner.

Thin stems (for flowers, Stained Glass and Celtic Appliqué [see page 104]) can be manufactured by cutting the required length of fabric on the cross at three times the finished width. Pass a pin through the cover of your ironing board so that the gap under it equals the finished width of the stem (Diagram 42). Then, turning both seam allowances under, pull the stem under the pin, ironing the folded fabric as it emerges. This is particularly worthwhile for patterns with a lot of stems! If the stems are curved, stab pin the stems into the required shape on the ironing board, then spray starch and steam press them. The stems will retain their curve, and any fullness on the inside of curves will be shrunk so that they lie flat.

Working on a table (not your knee because it could introduce curving), position the shapes according to the master plan and pin them onto the background fabric. Baste them. Work in sections so that shapes can be repositioned if necessary to compensate for any unexpected movement of some shapes. Because the seams do not need to match, appliqué is usually more

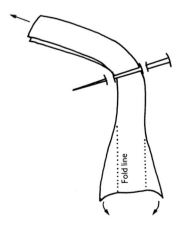

42 To make a stem, fold seam allowances under and pull under a pin. Then press

straightforward than piecing. However, for symmetrical patterns or highly complex ones, it is best to draw the picture onto the background as an aid in placing the appliqué.

To transfer these lines, place net (used for bridal veils or dancing costumes) over the master plan and trace the pattern on the net with a 2B pencil. The soft pencil marks the net and does not drag on it so that the net does not distort the picture. The net is then positioned on the backing fabric, and the lines are drawn over again with the pencil. This technique is especially useful for patterns based on circles. Work on a symmetrical pattern is made easier by laying threads across the backing fabric along the quarter and diagonal axes and sticky taping them at either end. These lines show the axes around which the appliqué shapes are arranged. Alternatively, these lines could be pressed into the background fabric. When the appliqué has been basted, these guide threads are then removed.

SEWING

The thread should match the top fabric, so you may need several colours. If you are working with a multicoloured print, choose a medium colour thread.

Starting with a knot at the back, bring the needle up through the fold of the appliquéd shape, then pass the needle down through the backing fabric slightly ahead of the point of emergence. This helps to make the stitch less obvious. Stitches should be less than 2 mm ($\frac{1}{8}$ in.) apart (Diagram 43a).

Firmly anchor any points. Trim the seam allowance to reduce bulk, sew up to the point and overstitch it. With the tip of the

Appliqué stitch

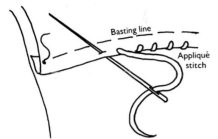

43a Hand appliqué

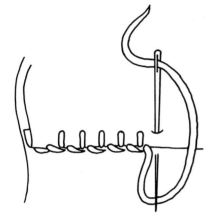

43b Blanket stitch

needle, tuck in the seam
allowance at right angles to the
point. Then fold in the seam
allowance of the descending side
and stitch, starting in the same
hole as the last stitch. This should
give a very sharp point.

To prevent unravelling where
the seam allowance has been
clipped at inner points, make a
series of tight stitches close
together. Always end a thread
with a knot or backstitch on the
back of the work.

Blanket stitch is an alternative
stitch for appliquéing if a
decorative effect is desired (43b).
Wendy Saclier and Vivienne
Mildren use this in *Memories*.

If you have covered a large area
of backing fabric in appliqué, the
backing fabric can be carefully
trimmed away, leaving a 5 mm
($\frac{1}{4}$ in.) seam allowance. This
leaves fewer layers for quilting.

Memories by Wendy Saclier and Vivienne Mildren. 192 cm x 155 cm (75½ in. x 61 in.).
Hand embroidery and blanket stitch appliqué. Hand quilted

MACHINE APPLIQUÉ

MARKING AND CUTTING

Unless you plan to turn the edge
under and secure the appliqué
with a straight stitch, machine
appliqué differs from hand
appliqué in one important
respect. Whereas a seam
allowance is necessary when
working by hand, none is required
if you are doing machine work.
There is no need to turn the seams
because the machine stitch locks
the edges and prevents them from
fraying.

Iron-on, double-sided Vilene is
used by some quiltmakers to
anchor the shape in place instead
of hand basting. While it is useful,
the Vilene often stiffens the fabric
and the long-term effect of the
glue used to bond the layers
together is not certain. On a piece
of clothing that is to be worn for
only a few seasons and then
discarded this may not matter,
but in a quilt that should last
many years it is best avoided.

SEWING

Satin stitch is usually used in
machine appliqué. Depending on
the effect you desire, the stitch
width can be made long so that
the stitching becomes a feature, or
short so that it is just long enough
to catch the appliqué. Val Moore

has used a short stitch width in carefully matched thread so the line of stitching is not conspicuous in her quilt, *The Flower Press* (see page 94). The most practical stitch length is between 0 and 1 as this stops any frayed threads escaping between the stitches.

As with hand appliqué, place the shapes in position and decide the order of sewing. Shapes that underlie others are sewn first and they are not sewn wherever they remain hidden.

To ensure that the appliqué does not pull out of the row of stitching, the zigzag stitch should always be perpendicular to the edge of the shape (Diagram 44). So on a curved edge it is necessary to stop with the needle still in the fabric, then to lift the presser foot and pivot the fabric to maintain this angle. On a concave edge, the needle should be left on the inside of the zigzag, on the convex edge it should be on the outside swing of the needle. This eliminates any gaps in the line of stitching.

Because satin stitch is so prominent, it may help the design to extend the line of stitching beyond the appliqué fabric across onto the background fabric. In the sample illustrated, I used the stitch not only to anchor the appliqué, but also to define the feathers of the bird.

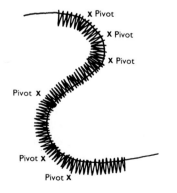

44 When machine appliquéing, always pivot the fabric so that the edge of the fabric is perpendicular to the zigzag stitch

Machine appliqué can be very strong and consequently is the best technique to use on clothing and cot quilts that will be frequently washed.

PRESSING

As a general rule, the seam allowances of appliquéd shapes are turned under the appliqué. This gives the shape a little height, raising it in importance. Because you want to keep this height, do not press too hard. Lay a fluffy towel on the ironing board and place the appliquéd work face down to press the seam allowances and remove any creases. Turn the work and press lightly on the right side.

As with most rules there are exceptions. When it is planned that the appliqué should recede into the background, press the seam allowances away from it, as Jennifer Lewis has done in *Cockies Naive* (see page 80).

QUILTING

As with pressing, the usual aim of the quilting is to make the appliqué stand up, so the shapes are usually quilted around in the ditch. Another line of quilting 5 mm ($\frac{1}{4}$ in.) further out packs down the background even more, isolating the appliqué. In traditional appliqué quilts large expanses of background were packed down with a regular filler pattern such as a cross-hatched grid (see Diagram 67 on page 127). This also emphasised the appliqué because the contrast between the straight quilting lines and the curved shapes made the curves stand out.

HAWAIIAN APPLIQUE

Hawaiian Appliqué was a local adaptation of the quiltmaking techniques brought to Hawaii by the early missionaries. This highly stylised representation of the luxurious flora on the island is very striking in appearance. With no accumulated scraps of material to use up, the Hawaiians used two or sometimes three layers of solid fabrics for each quilt. The top fabric is folded and cut to create a symmetrical design like a snowflake, while the background fabric is left whole as a foundation. Occasionally smaller pieces are appliqued on top of the snowflake layer.

MARKING AND CUTTING

You can use one of the traditional patterns or cut your own, first practising in paper. Start with a square of paper that is the same size as the finished quilt, fold it in half and then in quarters (Diagrams 45a and b). Fold on the diagonal (45c). The apex of this triangle is called the picot by Hawaiians. As the design is actually cut into the fabric it will be multiplied by the number of layers that have been folded together. Be careful not to sever the pieces by cutting the long folded edge or the design will fall apart when it is opened out. Vary the length of the points — if they are an equal distance from the edge of the square it will be less interesting than if some are short and some long. The paper left can itself become a pattern for Reverse Appliqué (see page 102).

Round off any inward points. It is possible to refold along slightly different lines, and recut to increase the complexity of the design.

Template construction

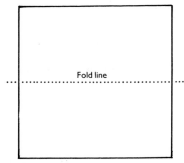

45a Construct a square and fold in half

45b Fold in quarters

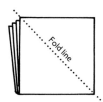

45c Fold in half again along the diagonal to form a triangle.

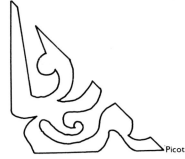

45d Cut the design into the folded paper. Carefully cut off the top layer of the folded paper which will now form the template

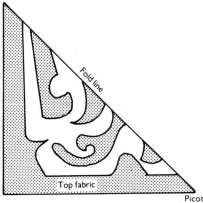

45e Place the template on the fabric that will form the top. This fabric will have been folded as described in 45a to c

Leave enough space around the cut-out snowflake design to show off later quilting on the background fabric. Alternatively, the border of the quilt can be made up from a border of Hawaiian Appliqué cut separately from the central feature. The outer edge parallels the background fabric, while the inner edge is folded, cut and then opens out to reveal the border pattern or lei.

Carefully cut off the top layer of the folded paper, which is one-eighth of the final design. This becomes the template for cutting out the design in fabric (45d). Fold the fabric as above (halves, quarters and on the diagonal). If printed fabric is used, the right sides should be folded together. Pin the paper template in position and trace the outline onto the

fabric (45e). Cut out the design, being careful not to move the layers of folded fabric. Stab pinning will anchor them.

HAND APPLIQUÉ

Fold the backing fabric as before, right sides together, and iron in the folds. Then spread out the backing fabric, right side up. Matching fold lines, lay the folded top along a quarter line, with the picot in the centre of the background fabric (Diagram 46a). Gently unfold the top, lining up the creases with the crease lines in the background fabric (46b, c and d). Every edge is on the bias, so avoid stretching the fabric. Pin baste and then thread baste at least 15 mm ($\frac{1}{2}$ in.) from the edge.

Hawaiian Appliqué is free flowing and does not show inaccuracies as obviously as geometric shapes. For this reason it is not necessary to first baste under seam allowances. Simply roll over a small amount of the fabric, say 3 mm ($\frac{1}{8}$ in.), using the point of the needle, and hand

Positioning the folded top on the backing fabric

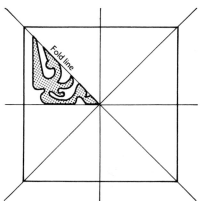

46a Place folded and cut top on backing fabric, matching crease lines and picots

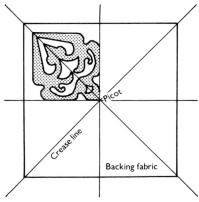

46b Unfold one layer of top, matching crease lines

46c Unfold next layer

46d Unfold last layer. Baste top to backing fabric and then appliqué into position

appliqué it. Fix points with an overstitch, 3 mm ($\frac{1}{8}$ in.) before the point, then turn under the next side. Snip the seam allowance of concave sides as required.

MACHINE APPLIQUÉ

Although Hawaiian Appliqué is worked by hand in most cases, it is possible to sew it by machine. Instead of folding the fabric to cut out the design, lay the opened-out paper pattern on the right side of the fabric that is stacked on top of the backing fabric and secured to it by basting thread. Transfer the design. Baste the top of the lining and sew along all the design lines. Trim the unwanted areas of the top fabric, being very careful not to snip the layer beneath. Now satin stitch this raw edge, enclosing the line of straight stitching. Use a thread that matches the colour of the top layer.

QUILTING

Hawaiian Appliqué is traditionally echo or contour quilted, with quilting lines surrounding the design of the top fabric and echoing its shapes. Sometimes the top fabric is quilted in a grid to contrast with the background.

DRESDEN PLATE

Appliqué and piecing can be combined in the same work. For instance, each block in Jennifer Lewis's *Cockies Naive* (see page 80) has a pieced curve background, onto which a cocky has been appliquéd. Alternatively, the appliqué shape itself may first be pieced before it is applied to the background fabric. A well-loved example of this is the Dresden Plate, and its construction is given below. The individual petals that make up the plate are first pieced, then the plate is appliquéd to the background.

In Dresden Plate the number of petals varies, and the ends of the petals can all be rounded, all pointed, or a combination of the two. The block in Susan McIver's sampler, *Carly's Quilt* (see page 65), has a combination, and 20 petals.

DRAFTING

Using the same centre point, describe two circles, one within the other, with a compass. Use a protractor to subdivide the larger circle into the chosen number of equal sectors (from 12 to 20). To obtain the rounded end of the sector ABO, bisect it (OC) and positioning the compass point on this midline, then move it up and down, drawing an arc that passes through A and B until the desired shape is found (Diagram 47). Cut out this segment with a curved outer edge and cut along the inner circle line. The resulting petal is the template.

If no compass is available, trace around household utensils, such as plates for the large circles and cups for the inner circle and petal ends. Cut around the outer circle. Carefully fold the circle in half again and again until a petal of the desired width is formed. Cut out one petal. Fold the petal in half lengthwise again, and cut a curve from the apex at the centre of the petal down to the lower edge. When the paper is unfolded this will give a rounded edge. For a point, just cut an angled straight line. The template for a petal is

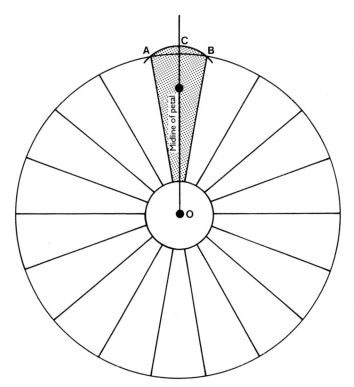

47 Draw two circles, one within the other. Construct segment lines by the same method explained in Diagrams 37a, b and c. From centre point 0 bisect one segment, then move compass point along this line to find point where an arc through point A and B forms the most pleasing petal end. Draw the arc to form the petal. Cut out template

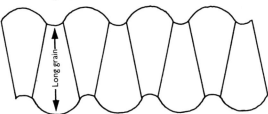

Position templates top to tail aligned with long grain

halfway in towards the centre so that the plate will lie flat (49b). Sew pairs of petals together, then pairs of pairs, and finally halves. Press all the seams in the same direction, say clockwise, so that later the quilting will be consistent. Fold backing fabric into quarters and press in fold lines.

Sewing Dresden Plate

49a Baste curved edges and clip concave seam allowance

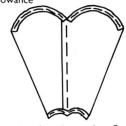

49b Sew pairs of petals together. Press seam allowances in same direction. Join all pairs to form plate

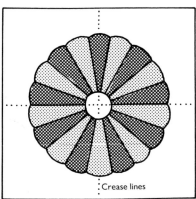

49c Centre Dresden Plate on crease lines of backing fabric. Baste and appliqué around inner circle and petal edges

the area between the recently cut outer edge and the original smaller circle which can now be cut off.

MARKING AND CUTTING

Make a template of the petal shape and mark in the midline and grain line. Lay the template on the wrong side of the fabric, matching the long grain with the midline and trace around the template. Turn the fabric over and retrace the curved ends. Position the fabric by sticking pins through from the back at either end of the curve. Cut 5 mm ($\frac{1}{4}$ in.) outside the line for the seam allowance. For machine piecing the petals, or making a whole quilt of Dresden Plate, make a template that includes the seam allowance. Mark the top layer of a stack of fabrics, flipping the template from top to tail so that a row of petals, all with midlines

aligned to the long grain, are marked (Diagram 48).

For hand sewing, marking is more complex than usual because Dresden Plate is pieced as well as appliquéd. Mark the long, straight sewing lines on the wrong side of the fabric, then put a pin through each end point. On the right side of the fabric, position the template so that it lies inside the four pins. Mark the top and bottom curves of the petal. These lines will be appliquéd.

If the petals are machine pieced and hand appliquéd, the straight lines need not be marked. In this case, place the template directly on the front and mark the curved sewing lines.

HAND APPLIQUÉ

Baste the curved edges (see Diagram 49a on page 102). Sew the petals together, stitching on the inside of the sewing line from

Centre the plate on the backing fabric (either an individual block or the whole quilt top), lining up a seam or the midline of a petal with the crease lines (49c). Baste. Appliqué, then remove the basting. Turn the block over and cut away the overlaying backing fabric to reduce the bulk, leaving a 5 mm ($\frac{1}{4}$ in.) seam allowance.

Press the seams towards the plate to make it stand out.

MACHINE AND HAND SEWING

The petals can be machined together after the curved edges have been basted. Start and end with a few stitches with a stitch length of nearly zero, so the stitches will not unravel.

The machine is also useful for sewing the pointed ends of petals. Right sides together, pin together the ends of the curve A and B. Sew from point AB to midpoint D, through all the seam allowances. Turn out the point and press.

Next, machine together the petals, leaving only the seam allowances at the bottom free so that the inner circle can be hand basted, then hand appliquéd. Continue to make up each block, and then press, as for hand appliqué.

QUILTING

Traditionally the Dresden Plates are lined up in rows, and the negative space of the background fabric forms a subsidiary pattern that is enhanced by a quilting pattern. The plates themselves are quilted in the ditch, with an extra line of quilting 5 mm ($\frac{1}{4}$ in.) away from the plate to puff up the appliqué. The circle in the centre of the plate may also be quilted in a design.

REVERSE APPLIQUÉ

Fabric stacked together, with the design actually cut into the material to reveal the underlying colours, is called Reverse Appliqué. Instead of applying pieces to a background fabric, the design is cut into the top layer, the seam turned under and sewn to the layer beneath.

The h'mong tribe of the hillsides of northern Thailand are renowned for their intricate Reverse Appliqué. Traditionally they used only two layers of fabric, with the top one usually being white. The patterns are geometric, and radiate towards the edges, often formed from central swirls surrounded by equally spaced lines. A positive/negative design is created with the striped effect of the contrast between the white top layer and the strong colour of the underlying fabric. The design evenly covers the surface area. The outer borders of the top fabric can be removed, so the lines of white form a pattern superimposed on the dark fabric without dominating it.

The skill of the work of the h'mong is shown by the closeness of the fine lines of fabric: the tiny seam allowances are turned under, leaving only very narrow white rows. As well, a little embroidery is sometimes used to break up larger areas of colour.

The San Blas islanders from Panama have also developed a technique of Reverse Appliqué to express their vibrant interpretations of their surroundings. Their *molas* are created from several layers of solid colour, with inserts of additional colour in some areas to increase the complexity of the work. The background areas are broken up into groups of strips. Each group could be a different colour, with that fabric being inserted under the top layer. Small appliquéd pieces complete the picture. The designs are frequently based on stylised birds and animals, although they can be exclusively geometric. Marjorie Coleman continues this tradition, basing her work on Australian flora and fauna in *San Blas Study 2*.

Any design will work, as long as the shapes are contained on all sides. In general it is better with *mola* to position the darkest fabrics on top so that seam allowances will not show as shadows, and so the outlines of any inserted patches cannot be seen. The varied fabric layers can be used to create designs of great beauty and intricacy, but more than five layers becomes difficult to handle.

Aboriginal designs with groups of stripes breaking up the background also lend themselves to Reverse Appliqué.

HAND APPLIQUÉ

Reverse Appliqué is traditionally hand worked to ensure that the stitching is not obvious. Select fabrics that hold a crease well and that do not bulk up. Pure cotton is usually a good choice for this reason. Because you do not cut into the bottom layer, a more difficult fabric can be used there. If a foundation fabric is also used, one with a thin, open weave, such as cheesecloth, will increase the bulk least. Because only thin strips of most colours show, fabric is usually confined to solids. If you choose to use a print, however, consider how it will appear in small sections. A very close print will read more consistently than a large print

San Blas Study No. 1 by Marjorie Coleman. 60 cm x 50 cm (23½ in. x 19½ in.). Reverse appliqué by hand

which may reveal quite different colours and shapes from one area to the next. Allow at least 2.5 cm (1 in.) extra around the design — this extra fabric can act as a border. The design is transferred to the top layer by using a light-table, which can be created by shining a table lamp up through a glass-topped table or by taping the design and fabric to a sunlit window so that the lines show through. If the top layer is black, the design can be transferred with netting. Place the netting on the

pattern and trace over the lines with a soft lead pencil. Position the netting onto the black fabric and trace over the pencil markings with a white pencil or thin chalk. When the netting is removed, the dotted pattern left on the fabric can be drawn over again if it is not clear enough. Then stack the layers in the order in which they will be revealed, aligning the grains. Thread baste around the margin.

The top layer is cut between the design lines and the seams are

folded back under to the design line with the point of the needle, and then appliquéd down. Use a thread in a colour that matches the top layer. Snip any inner points and stitch closely to prevent fraying.

Next, cut into the second layer down, appliquéing the edges so that it appears as a strip circling the third layer. Continue this process until the bottom layer is revealed. If this is repeated layer by layer, a series of narrow bands will be left. If you decide, as part of your design, to skip several layers, all the layers above the fabric to be revealed are cut, and the seam allowances of all but the top one can be trimmed to reduce the bulk.

Working with too many layers can be difficult to handle so, if a colour is only being used in one portion of the design, insert a patch in that colour between the layers in the relevant area. Fabric shapes can also be appliquéd onto the top layer to give the impression that another layer has been almost entirely cut away.

QUILTING

Because of all the layers involved, this technique is often left unquilted. The bulk of several layers substitutes for batting. If you wish to quilt, plan the quilting lines in areas where most layers have been cut away.

STAINED GLASS AND CELTIC APPLIQUÉ

The effect of stained-glass windows has been transferred to appliqué by laying together fabric pieces in a design and covering the joins with bias tape, often black to suggest the lead used to hold stained glass together. Indeed the designs of these windows can frequently be an inspiration (Diagram 50). American Roberta Horton applied this technique to fabric for a quilting class and later wrote about it. The different ways that glass reflects the light can be simulated by using slightly varying shades and textures of the same colour. Even if the same

fabric is used, you can change the effect by running the grain in a different direction.

A variation on this technique is Celtic Appliqué. Drawing on her Irish origins, Philomena Wiechec was inspired by the Celtic interlace designs to be found in Gospel books such as *The Book of Kells* and other illuminated manuscripts of the tenth century, as well as by metal designs and woodwork, and has developed them into quilt patterns. As in Stained Glass, the bias strips outline the shapes, but in working with fabric the designs are usually symmetrical with a radial development. The bias strips are a feature, used to form intricate knots, scrolls and borders. Ann Lhuede's *Celtic Keys* is a fine example.

The technique of Reverse Appliqué can also be used to create the effect of stained glass, with the top layer being black to form the outlining strips.

MARKING AND CUTTING

Draft the design with a black felt-tip pen so that when it is overlaid with the foundation fabric the lines will show through enough to be traced onto the fabric. Number each piece. Retain the master pattern and make templates, numbering them according to the master. Cut the fabric slightly larger than the finished size so that gaps will not appear between the pieces if there is some movement during sewing.

The bias strips should be made from pure cotton because this holds creases well and presses into shape easily. As the bias strips used in Stained Glass are usually short, it is not necessary to make continuous bias. To cut the bias tape for shorter lengths, cut strips on the diagonal that are three

50 Stained Glass Designs
(Source: Sibbett, 1977)

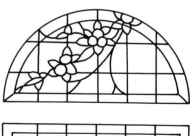

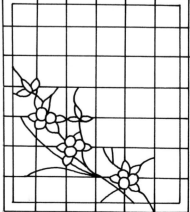

Celtic Keys by Ann Lhuede. 220 cm x 190 cm (86½ in. x 75 in.). Hand pieced, appliquéd and quilted

times the finished width, then iron both seam allowances towards the back. In Celtic Appliqué, however, the strips are longer so see page 143 for instructions to make continuous bias binding. Of course, you can always buy it! For longer lengths, the method for making thin stems on page 96 can be used.

If a sharp curve is to be sewn, prepare the bias tape by pinning it on the ironing board in the desired curve, then spray starch and steam press. The excess puckers on the concave side will disappear and the fabric will retain the required shape, making sewing easier.

HAND APPLIQUÉ

Position the pieces onto the design marked out on the foundation fabric, with the edges slightly overlapping. Plan which bias strips will lie under the others. These can be cut first, and their cut ends will be concealed by other bias strips. Position the bias strips along the design lines, concealing the edges of the fabric shapes. Pin baste, then thread baste. Hand appliqué all the bias strips.

QUILTING

Stained Glass patchwork and Celtic Appliqué are usually quilted in the ditch.

CLAMSHELLS

The clamshell shape has appeared in the needlework of many cultures; in Japan, for example, it is known as "fish scales" and often occurs in *sashiko*, a form of Japanese quilting. The Clamshell design is used in patchwork tops as well as being a motif in quilting. Clamshell

51 Arrangements of Clamshells

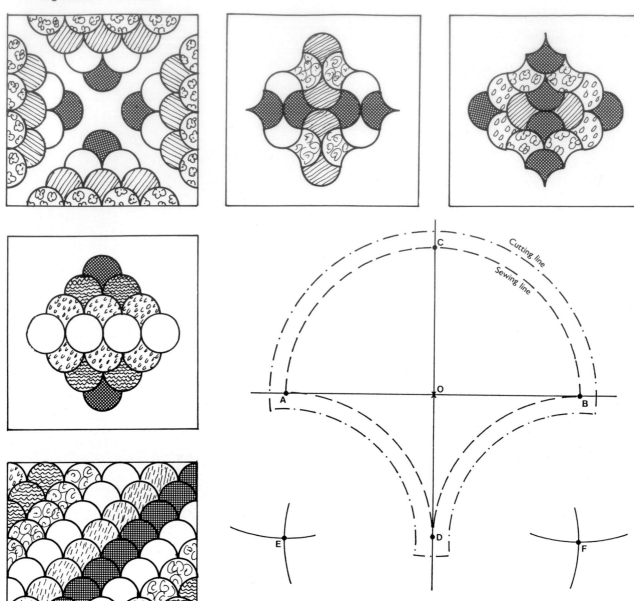

52 Drafting Clamshells
Draw two lines at right angles and describe a circle using intersection of lines as point 0. With compass point first on A and them on D, describe arcs to form intersection at E. With compass point on E describe arc through A and D. Repeat on adjacent side to find arc DB. Clamshell is now complete. Add seam allowances

blocks appear in the sampler quilt by Susan McIver (see page 65).

In patchwork the repeat shape may be sewn in rows to cover the quilt top, the rows can be confined to fill a single block, or the shape can be rotated to develop a medallion pattern (Diagram 51).

DRAFTING

Draft directly onto the template so that the curves do not have to be transferred. Draw a line longer than the diameter of the circle required. Next, draw another line at right angles to the first. Describe a circle of the required diameter centred on the

intersection of the lines (point 0 on Diagram 52). These will intersect the circle at AB and CD. If the clamshells have to fit across a particular length of backing fabric, make sure that the diameter of the circle divides evenly into the length so that the clamshells will fit exactly.

Using the same radius, bisect

two adjacent quarters. With the compass point on intersection E draw an arc connecting A and D. Repeat with the compass point on F: the arc should pass through D and B. The clamshell is now complete. At the "stalk" the arcs appear to converge before they meet the point. To ease sewing, redraw the arcs so that they end a few millimetres on either side of D.

MARKING AND CUTTING

Place the template on the right side of the fabric with the grain line running up through the shape. Trace around the shape. The choice of fabric colours and prints will determine the final overall pattern, even though the same shape is repeated.

Cut around the shape leaving a seam allowance of 5 mm ($\frac{1}{4}$ in.). Baste under the top curve and any other side that overlies another piece in the final design (Diagram 53). Concave curves need to be clipped in the seam allowance.

53 Basting a clamshell

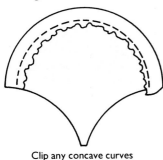

Clip any concave curves

HAND APPLIQUÉ

To position the clamshells correctly, stab pin the shapes into position on an ironing board, or a cork or styrene board (Diagram 54a). This way a piece will not be moved accidentally when another nearby is relocated. If an entire quilt top is being formed from rows of clamshells, pin the shapes

Positioning rows and medallions of clamshells

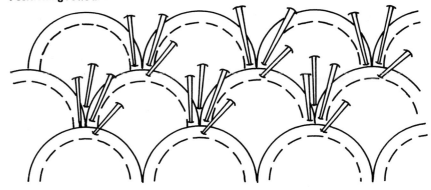

into the carpet and make sure that the rows are straight and parallel. A string stretched across to denote the top of the row will act as a guideline for straightening the rows. Start at the top and move it down for each new row. Position each row over the seam allowances of the one above.

Ensure that the points intersect cleanly, with basted edges overlying the seam allowances of adjacent clamshells. The clamshells should be lined up so that they converge at the point of the stalk (D) above. Where four corners come together in a medallion the seam allowances are folded together like the sides of a carton (54b). If two stalks meet, the end seam allowance of the stalk on top is folded under.

Pin baste the shapes together and then remove the stab pins and lift the connected clamshells. Thread baste, sewing from the top corner where there are few pins. Hand appliqué.

When the clamshells are sewn together, lay them on the backing fabric, centring them carefully. Pin baste, then thread baste. When they have been hand appliquéd onto the background, remove all the basting threads (see Diagram 55 on page 108). To make quilting easier, cut out the overlaid backing fabric, leaving a 5 mm ($\frac{1}{4}$ in.) seam allowance. Be careful not to accidentally snip the top layer.

54a (above) Position and stab pin clamshells in rows. Pin baste, then thread baste together

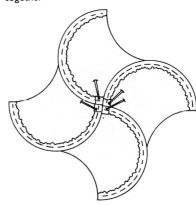

54b A medallion of clamshells with edges carefully aligned. Seam allowances folded carton fashion. Stab pin, pin baste and then thread baste

MACHINE APPLIQUÉ

In machine appliqué the positioning of the clamshells dictates whether the seam allowance is included or left off. Only those sides that lie under others need a seam allowance. Be sure to pivot the fabric under the needle so that the zigzag stitch is perpendicular to the edge or too little fabric will be caught under the stitch and it could fray in time (see the general section on Machine Appliqué on page 97).

BORDER

A clamshell border on a quilt can look effective. Face the clamshells for the bottom row by hand or machine before sewing the several

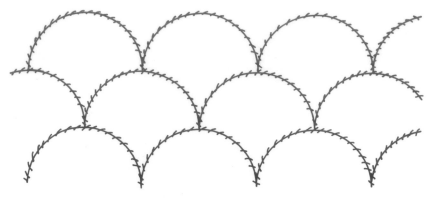

55 Hand appliqué clamshells together, sew onto backing fabric then remove basting thread

rows together. To face them, sew two clamshells, right sides together, along the top curve. Trim the seam allowances. Turn right side out and press.

QUILTING

Clamshells are traditionally quilted in the ditch. If the shapes are very large, several lines of quilting could parallel the top curve.

CRAZY PATCH

The Crazy Patch quilt may have been born of the necessity to use up every scrap of fabric to make bedding, but in the hands of the women of the Victorian era it became an opportunity to show off a variety of luxurious fabrics, from silks to velvets, all sewn onto a foundation fabric and richly embroidered. Beautified with beads, ribbons and other embellishments, the quilts were hardly practical bedcoverings, but were displayed as piano covers, cushions, and other decorations. Wendy Saclier's *Miniature Victorian Crazy* comes from this tradition. Marjorie Coleman's *Townhouse* (see page 16) is a more contemporary version.

MARKING AND CUTTING

Crazy Patch quilts are usually sewn in blocks and then the blocks are assembled to make the quilt. Cut foundation blocks of the required size (40 cm or 15 in. is often practical) from a stable fabric that is easy to needle. This fabric will not be seen in the finished quilt, so you could use old shirting, bedding or cheap cotton.

The Crazy Patch can include velvets, silks, cottons, blends, synthetics, textured fabrics, satins, or pieces of sentimental value, perhaps from a wedding dress, old ties, or ribbons. Because of the combination of fabrics it is unlikely that the finished article could ever go through the washing machine.

HAND PIECING

There is no initial design as the effect is developed by the combination of textures and colours, and may be determined by the size of the scraps available. Starting in one corner, place a fabric so that it covers the edges of the foundation block. Place other fabrics, allowing a generous overlap, and play around with the pieces until the effect is pleasing.

Make sure that any fabric likely to fray is overlaid on all edges.

Traditionally, raw edges were left exposed, as all edges are later embroidered, but it is more common these days to turn under seam allowances. Because velvet is bulky if a seam is turned, it is better to place it under other fabrics. Check that the foundation fabric will not be exposed by gaps. To conceal all edges, use Log Cabin construction as explained below.

MACHINE PIECING

The construction is in Log Cabin style. After arranging the fabrics in a pleasing manner, take two adjacent pieces and machine them together, right sides facing, sewing, at the same time, through to the foundation fabric if you are using one. Turn the top fabric back and press. Sew on the next piece that joins them. It may be easier to trim the edges, right sides together, before sewing. Press at each stage. The edges are all turned under in this method, so embroidery is optional.

Wendy Holland achieves a Crazy Patch effect, but not by building it up piece by piece. Using the sewing machine for speed and because the lines of stitching can be cut through (hand piecing would unravel), she sews large pieces of fabric together, then cuts through the resulting piece. She turns sections upside down, inserts extra fabrics, cuts and resews several times. As they are cut and resewn, the patches of each fabric become smaller and smaller, and the overall picture more complex. At each stage she considers the balance of colours, prints and shapes.

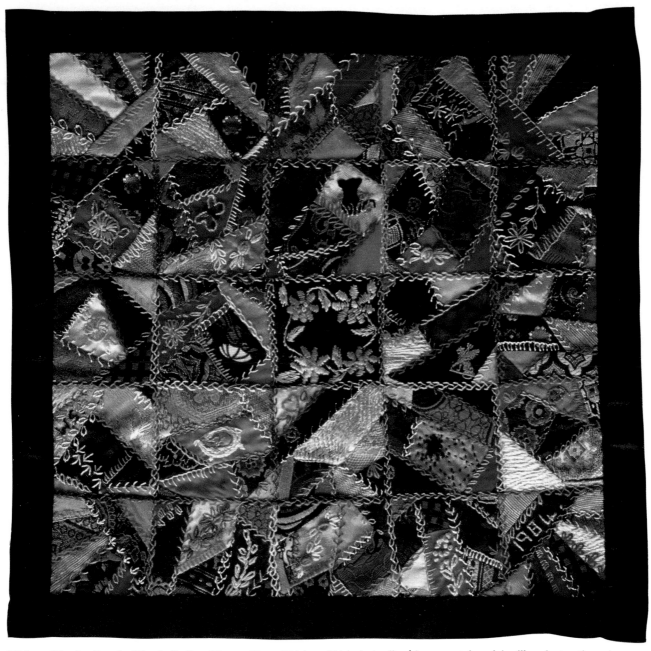

Miniature Victorian Crazy by Wendy Saclier. 22 cm x 22 cm (8½ in. x 8½ in.). Appliquéd crazy patchwork in silk, velvet, satin and taffeta. Embellished with traditional embroidery stitches

QUILTING AND EMBROIDERY

Embroidery rather than quilting was the feature of many old Crazy Patch quilts; they were lined, but no batting was included. As their primary function was decorative, warmth was not required.

For hand embroidery use perle embroidery thread and decorative stitches. Sew over all the seams, making certain that the foundation is caught. Some of the stitches available are illustrated on page 165. Prue Socha has provided some examples of the more useful ones (see page 110).

The colour of the thread should contrast strongly with the fabrics being sewn, otherwise the effect is lost. Different colours can be used, black and gold thread are particularly striking.

Embroidered motifs and pictures can also be worked into the patches. According to Margaret Rolf's research, sprays of wattle, birds, insects, spiderwebs and other objects were typical of Victorian Crazy Patch in Australia.

Machine embroidery is also

Samples of embroidery stitches by Prue Socha

Rose Window by Megan Terry.
275 cm x 275 cm (108 in. x 108 in.).
Hand pieced by English Paper Method

very effective. The machine fancy stitch can be varied from one seam to another. The thread ends should be taken to the back and knotted to prevent unravelling.

These days, when Crazy Patch is often sewn with dress-weight fabrics for clothing or bed quilts, a batting is often included and the quilt is quilted along the seam lines. Hand or machine embroidery stitches can be used to quilt.

ENGLISH
PAPER METHOD

Many first quilts are hexagon quilts, pieced together using the English Paper Method. The finished shape is cut out in paper

and the fabric is basted over it. The hexagons are then sewn together. This a very precise method of construction, but more time consuming because of the extra step involved. As its name implies, the technique originated in England (Colby, 1982), and is still very popular there. The method can be used for any pieced block, and some quiltmakers even use the paper templates for appliqué, but it is most commonly used for hexagons.

The hexagon is a one-patch, and colours can be randomly placed or they can be organised. Rosettes are the most common arrangement, and Grandmother's Flower Garden (see page 163) is the most common pattern deriving from rosettes. In this, the central hexagon is surrounded by two circles of hexagons, then all the rosettes are joined with a solid

colour hexagon forming the garden path between them. A stripe can look very effective, although the stripe must line up neatly with an adjoining hexagon in the same striped fabric. Megan Terry arranges rosettes into her magnificent *Rose Window*.

The six-sided figure can also be arranged into a star pattern, or be drawn out into a diamond effect. Nancy Tingey uses the shape to build up a picture, changing the colours to suggest a particular effect in *Search for School Grey* (see page 12).

DRAFTING

The size of the basic circle determines the size of the hexagon. Describe a circle, then draw a line AB passing through the centre (point O) and both sides of the circle. With the compass the width of the radius and its point on A, mark the radius on the circle on both sides C and D. With the compass point on B, mark the intersections E and F. The circle is now evenly divided into six. To check the accuracy of the drafting, place the compass point on B and intersect the circle. The intersection should pass through E and F. Join AC, CE, EB, BF, FD, DA to complete the hexagon (Diagram 56).

Another popular design based on the hexagon is Baby Blocks or Tumbling Blocks. Using the drafting above, join OF to give the diamond OFDA. Join OE to give the other two diamonds OEBF and OACE (Diagram 57). Traditionally the three diamonds are coloured light, medium and dark, consistently placed in each hexagon. This gives a three-dimensional effect, with the impression of a constant light source. Alison Muir's *Executive Ladder* (see page 112) shows how effective it can look. A three-dimensional effect can also be achieved by cutting the hexagon in half and arranging pairs of light, medium and dark fabrics (Diagram 58). Susan McIver uses this Inner City arrangement in *Carly's Quilt* (see page 65).

MARKING AND CUTTING

A window template is often useful in the English Paper Method. This is a template of the seam allowance, with the centre, the actual size of the piece, cut out. It can be placed accurately over a feature of the fabric, and both the sewing and cutting lines can then be traced off it. However, these days the plastic template material is transparent, so correct placement on a specific feature is not a problem, and the template can be the finished size, without seam allowance.

Use this template to cut many paper templates. The paper must be strong enough to retain its shape without being too tough to pass a needle through. Pin the paper template to the fabric aligning one side with the grain line. Cut around it leaving a seam allowance just less than 5 mm ($\frac{1}{4}$ in.). If a feature of the fabric is being picked out, place the plastic template over it and trace around it first in pencil, to give a guideline for the paper template.

SEWING

Baste the seam allowances of the hexagon over the paper, starting with a side on the grain line and the knot on the right side. Each side is folded and basted in turn working around in the same direction so that each point is a right angle. Secure the end of the thread by backstitching.

Once the placement for the particular pattern is determined, take two hexagons and sew them together. The position of the knots is a constant reminder of the grain line. In general, keep the grain line of all the hexagons running in the same direction. However, if a particular feature of the fabric is being used, the grain line can be discounted.

With right sides together and using a matching thread, whipstitch the two hexagons along the side where they meet, starting and stopping exactly on the corner (Diagram 59). The whipstitch catches the minimum amount of fabric and avoids the paper template so it can be released easily when the basting is removed later on. Join the next hexagon to these two, bearing in mind the direction of the grain line. Start and finish on the same

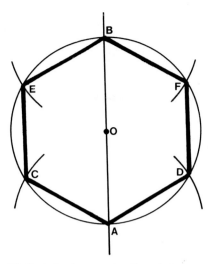

56 To draft a hexagon describe a circle around point 0. Draw a line AB passing through point 0 and edges of circle. From A draw arcs to find C and D. Repeat from B to find E and F. Join AC, CE, EB, BF, FD and DA

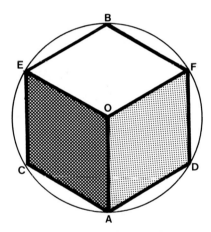

57 To construct a Baby Block, draft a hexagon as in Diagram 56. Then also join E0, F0 and A0

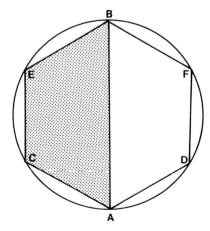

58 For Inner City draft a hexagon as in Diagram 56. AB divides hexagon into two templates

Executive Ladder by Alison Muir. 38 cm x 40 cm (15 in. x 15½ in.). Hand and machine pieced. Hand appliquéd. Machine quilted. Baby Blocks variation

stitches so that there are no holes in the corners.

If you are making rosettes, cut out a lot of pieces before deciding the final placement. Working in these small units keeps the work portable, and allows the arrangement to be flexible. When larger areas are sewn together, press and then remove the basting stitches to release the papers. The outside papers are only removed after they have all been pressed so

that the seam allowance is firmly turned into position and the whole work is ready to be sewn to a backing fabric. Centre the work on the background and then appliqué it down.

A very attractive border can be made by running rows of hexagons around the edge of the rosettes to create a swag effect. In this case the edge hexagons must each be backed by another hexagon, wrong sides together,

and whipstitched around three edges. The lining is trimmed to the outline of the edge of the quilt top and inserted between the faced hexagons so that no raw edges are exposed. Appliqué the last three sides of the backing hexagons onto the lining. Nancy Tingey finishes her hexagon quilts in that manner so that there is nothing to distract from the hexagons.

59 After cutting paper templates, pin to fabric and cut around them, adding seam allowances. Baste fabric over paper templates. Then, right sides together, whipstitch one edge of two hexagons together. Continue to form pattern

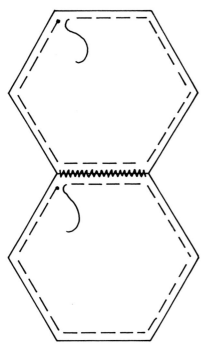

60 Hexagons can also be machine stitched together, abutting edges

MACHINE SEWING

The English Paper Method is most often sewn by hand, but it is possible to abut two edges of the basted shapes and run them through the sewing machine using a tiny zigzag stitch (Diagram 60). Keep the stitch width narrow so that it is less obvious. Finish off the threads by knotting them.

QUILTING

Unlike other piecing, the seam allowances in this method are pressed apart. For this reason quilting was traditionally done 5 mm ($\frac{1}{4}$ in.) inside the seam line to avoid the extra thickness. Sometimes the papers were enclosed in the quilt for extra warmth, and such pieces now provide an opportunity to date the work as well as to take an intimate glimpse into the life of the quiltmaker. Old letters, newspapers, and even wills were cut up to make the piecing papers. Early quilts made by this method were often not interlined with a batt, and instead of being quilted, may have been tied to the lining occasionally to prevent shifting.

LATTICES AND BORDERS

Lattices provide a grid to isolate individual blocks. They can be a major element in the design, as in Wendy Holland's *Java Quilt* (see page 114) and in Mae Bolton's *Boston Common's* (see page 33), or used merely as a form of division. Sampler quilts often use lattices to bring together disparate block designs. The lattices act like borders for each block in a quilt (see Diagram 61 on page 114).

The use of a border in the overall effect needs to be considered carefully. The border can be pieced (see Diagram 62a on page 115), appliquéd (62b), quilted (62c), or plain. Some quilts are enhanced by their use while others would appear rigidly contained if they were surrounded. A narrow binding is all that is needed to contain the richness of Wendy Saclier's *Miniature Victorian Crazy* (see page 109).

A plain border can frame a quilt and provide an area to show off the quilting. Barbara Ward's *Bush Window* (see page 40) exemplifies this. In another fashion Maree Gebhardt creates a border, without changing the quilt construction, by running a single colour through the Cathedral Windows around the edge of *Integrated Diamond*. Valerie Gordon has achieved a similar effect in *Kaleidoscope* (see page 35).

Borders can also be pieced: Elva Hine's *Floral Heirloom* (see page 94) has a pieced border that isolates the wonderful appliqué, and Susan McIver used strips of the darker fabrics to create a border for her Log Cabin *Lollipop Lane* (see page 74). The corners are filled by Courthouse Steps, which neatly turns the direction of the strips. In *1000 Hours* Jeanette Parsons (see page 94) created a border that makes a link with her appliquéd wreaths by taking the flowers and organising them in a row. She carefully planned the corners so that the design is mitred. A thin strip of dark green fabric sets the border apart from the central blocks, and this is echoed in the binding.

61 Lattices

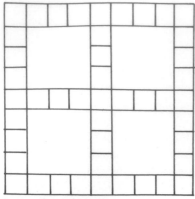

Lattice of pieced squares

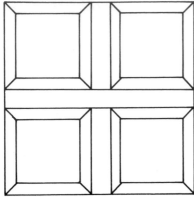

Lattice with window sashes

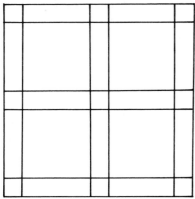

Lattice with corners

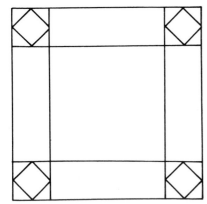

Lattice with pieced corners

Java Quilt by Wendy Holland. 193 cm x 193 cm (76 in. x 76 in.). Machine pieced. Hand quilted

In *Cockies Naive* (see page 80) Jennifer Lewis used the curved strips of the background in the blocks in the border, but by changing the tone in the stripped curves from the bottom to the top of the quilt, she implies the weight of the earth below and the airiness of the sky above.

The border can also be a major element in the overall design. My *Basket Quilt* was designed for a high iron bed, and, to eliminate any unsightly rucking of the corners when they are tucked into the bed end, I designed a block that sits on its point, alternating with plain blocks, and then arranged the blocks so that they created a border. In the bottom corners of the quilt, the plain blocks are eliminated, and two basket blocks sit together, so the border of baskets turns the corner,

allowing a large triangle of plain fabric to be left out. This reduced the bulk while still allowing the quilt to read well. A commercial stencil was used for the quilting design, and elements of it were turned and used to create a border of quilted swags around the edge of the quilt.

The secret to success in making borders is to ensure that they complement the patchwork design and do not overshadow it. The scale of the border and the strength of the colours should be carefully considered. The other factor to consider is the corners: to be unobtrusive they should turn neatly. This may require careful drafting but is essential to the harmony of the quilt. Only in a deceptively casual quilt such as Wendy Holland's *Pale Ladies* (see page 146) is this detailed planning

Borders

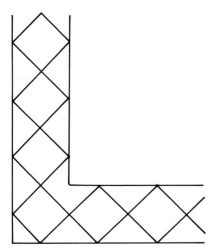

62a Pieced border

62b Appliqué border

62c Quilted border

Basket Quilt by Dianne Finnegan and Robyn Thornton. 280 cm x 280 cm (110 in. x 110 in.). Machine pieced. Hand quilted

unnecessary, and even here the overall effect has been carefully handled.

SEWING

Attaching the border provides an opportunity to bring the quilt back to a rectangle format if it has by chance grown in one direction. If all your measuring and sewing has been accurate this will not prove to be a problem, but occasionally a quilt does distort. Nothing looks worse than a rippling quilt hanging on the wall or in an exhibition, with corners

that are obviously not at right angles. Keep such a quilt on a bed!

Measure the quilt along the quarter lines from edge to edge, rather than along the sides, which might have stretched. Cut borders to fit these measurements, including seam allowances. If the border is to have a bound edge, this edge will have no seam allowance.

Pin and quarter the border and the side to which it is being attached. That is, find the centre point of the side of the border by folding it, and mark it with a pin.

Corner treatment for borders

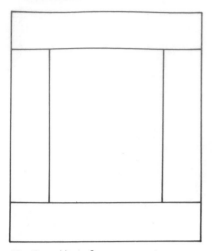

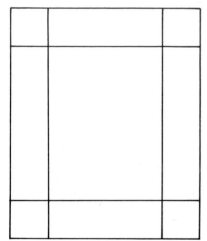

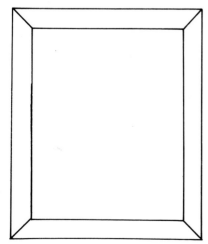

63a Court House Steps construction

63b Isolated corners

63c Mitred corners

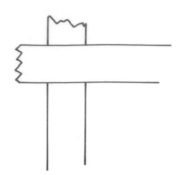

63d To mitre a corner extend borders beyond quilt

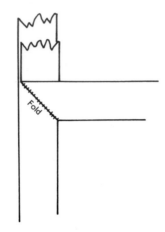

63e Fold top extension of border to form 45° angle to the side border. Appliqué and trim excess fabric

side borders, then the top and bottom, being careful to start and finish the lines of sewing exactly at the end of the sewing line. Do not sew through the seam allowance. Press top and bottom borders, then fold under the top and bottom borders to form 45° angles with the side borders (63e). Appliqué them in place. Turn to the back and trim away the excess fabric, leaving a seam allowance.

FABRIC MANIPULATION

Most quilts depend on varying the size and type of print in the fabric to achieve the impression of visual texture, with only the indentation of the quilting line to give a suggestion of a sculptural effect. However, instead of merely using the flat surface of the fabric, some quiltmakers have expanded their techniques and fold, tuck, twist or in some way manipulate fabric to achieve a sculptural, three-dimensional effect in their work.

This is not an entirely new direction; there have, in the past, been quilts that have relied on some of these methods, but it is only in recent years that they have been further explored and pushed beyond the confines of the bed quilt. Cathedral Window is a traditional folded technique that is still popular which Marie Gebhardt, in *Integrated Diamond*, has freshly interpreted by developing the pattern through the placement of the window fabrics.

Helen Gritscher gives new life to Puff Patchwork by using shiny fabrics, and stuffing only some of the shapes. Adèle Outteridge has also experimented with fabric

Repeat at the quarter points. Do the same to the side of the quilt, then pin the border to it, matching up the pins. Distribute any fullness evenly, then pin together and sew.

If the borders are being added in the Courthouse Steps style, sew the side borders first, then the top and bottom (Diagram 63a).

Isolated corners are another possibility. These can be in a different fabric or contain a block pattern (63b).

For mitred corners (63c), cut the border with a 45° angle extending beyond the quilt. Attach all the borders, then sew out along the mitres. An alternative method is to extend the border by its own width beyond the quilt (63d). Sew the

manipulation on a miniature scale, to push the work into an art form to be hung on the wall rather than covering a bed. She gathers, tucks, slashes, exposes raw edges, all in her exploration of colour and design using textiles.

Some of these techniques can be used for bed quilts. They are often constructed so that quilting is optional; because the fabrics are folded, their thickness gives extra warmth.

CATHEDRAL WINDOW

Cathedral Window quilts are usually composed of squares, which can be used in a variety of sizes to create optical illusions in which the design seems to bulge in some places and recede in others. Other basic shapes can include hexagons, coffin shapes or diamonds.

Because the method requires folding the fabric, pure cotton is preferable because it holds a fold better than a blend. The background fabric is traditionally calico, but any fabric can be used because little of it will show. The windows are so small that they can be cut out of scraps.

The following instructions apply to the basic square shape. Starting with a perfect square four times the finished size, plus seam allowance (see Diagram 64a on page 118), fold it in half, right sides together, matching seam lines. Sew up the side seams, by hand or machine (64b). Pull the midpoints of the open seams apart so that the sewn seams meet (64c). Pin together the seam allowances that are now opposed. Leaving a gap of about 4 cm ($1\frac{1}{2}$ in.) across the centre, sew out from the middle to each end.

Integrated Diamond by Maree Gebhardt. 280 cm x 280 cm (110 in. x 110 in.). Hand and machine sewn. Not quilted. Cathedral Window

Turn the piece inside out, to the right side, pushing the fabric through the gap. Stitch the gap closed using hand appliqué or whipstitch (64d). Press the shapes into a square. Working on an ironing board, stab pin each corner into the centre and press well, then remove the pins. Fold opposite corners to meet in the centre and anchor together with a few stitches (64e). Because the stitches will show, use matching thread and stitch neatly by hand.

Next, hold two of the folded squares together, right sides facing, and whipstitch along one edge (64f). Repeat, sewing squares into rows, then sewing rows together. The window square will sit on its point over the whipstitched line, its edges almost reaching the four foldlines of two adjacent folded squares (64g). Place the window in position,

then pull the folded edge down over it so that it curves over the cut edge. Pin in place and repeat with each side. Appliqué these folded edges in place, matching the thread to the top fabric. It now appears as a diamond shape enclosed in background fabric.

Not every window will need squares — their placement depends on the effect you want to achieve (64h). If the edges of the Cathedral Window block are also to contain windows, fold the windows in half, wrong sides together, and place the fold slightly over the the edge of the block so that when it is appliquéd down the block underneath does not show through.

The whole piece can be appliquéd to a backing fabric. This is particularly effective if it is to be set on the point in a sampler quilt. If thickness is a problem,

Cathedral Window

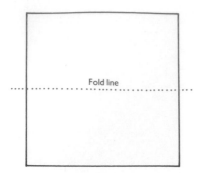

64a Cut square (first fold line shown)

64b Fold square in half. Stitch down sides

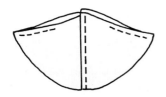

64c Pull centre points out to each side and stitch, leaving a gap in middle

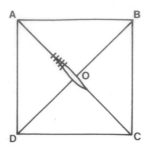

64d Pull fabric through gap to right side, forming a square. Stitch gap closed

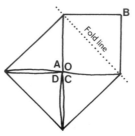

64e Fold down corners to meet at centre. Stitch together opposite points

64f Whipstitch squares together

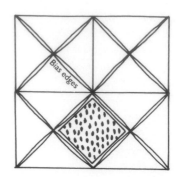

64g Place windows across join between two squares. Fold bias edges of square back over window. Pin baste and stitch

64h Completed Cathedral Window

the overlaid backing fabric can be trimmed away, leaving a seam allowance. Another idea for a whole quilt top made in this technique and then set on the point is to have a sawtooth edge (see page 143), with the individual cathedral windows forming the sawtooth. In this case do not turn back the outer folds.

PUFF QUILTS

Like Cathedral Window, Puff Quilts depend on their construction for warmth, and need not be quilted when the top is put together. Each individual

unit is stuffed with batting to give the puffed appearance. To accommodate the batting, the top square of each unit is larger than the backing square. Helen Gritscher's Puff Quilt, *Poppies Too*, is a fresh interpretation of this traditional technique. Athough it is based on a regular grid, some individual squares as well as some sets of squares are left unpuffed.

The backing squares will not be seen, so you can use any fabric to make them. The top square is cut about 2 cm ($\frac{3}{4}$ in.) larger than the one underneath (Diagram 65a). To make the lengths of the sides of the top square equal to those of the bottom square, fold the excess

fabric of the top over at the midpoint of each edge and pin (65b). Then, wrong sides together, pin the corners of the top and bottom squares together. Machine or hand sew one side. With top sides facing, stitch units together along the sides that are perpendicular to the first sewing line to produce rows of pockets. The top edge of each pocket or puff is left open to insert the stuffing (65c). Remove the pins and stuff each puff. The amount of batting will determine how puffy the square is. Fold and pin the excess fabric in each square (65d). Right sides together, sew the rows together, thus closing

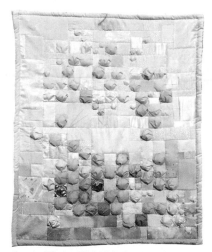

Poppies Too by Helen Gritscher. 96 cm x 79 cm (38 in. x 31 in.). Machine pieced. Hand quilted. Puff quilt

Assembling a Puff Quilt

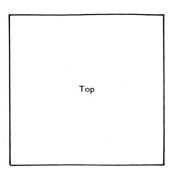

65a Smaller backing and larger top squares

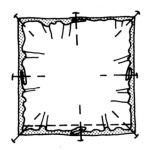

65b Pin larger top square to backing square, folding in excess fabric. Stitch along one edge

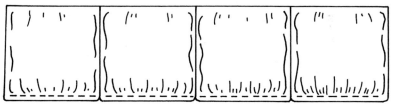

65c Sew puffs into rows to create pockets

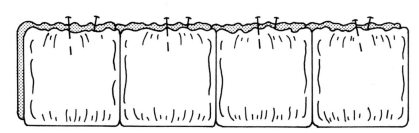

65d Stuff the pockets, pin in excess fabric and sew rows together to close puffs

each puff. Finish the last row.

All the seam allowances are on the back, so the quilt will need to be lined. The lining can be attached by putting the right sides of the top and lining together and sewing almost all the way round. Turn the quilt right side out and hand sew the final gap closed. Alternatively, the top and lining can be laid wrong sides together and the edges bound (65e). A large Puff Quilt will need to be tied to keep the layers from shifting.

SUFFOLK PUFFS

Made from many different fabrics, the 1930s Suffolk Puff Quilt pictured on page 120 is typical of its time. The quilt is composed of circles of fabric that have been gathered up. The circles are then joined in rows. Like working with hexagons, Puff Quilts are very portable while the individual puffs are being made. It is only when they are all sewn together that the work becomes bulky. This kind of patchwork is not quilted, and because the top of a Suffolk Puffs quilt does not give a continuous cover, the

bedspread underneath it shows through. There is no backing fabric.

Using a circle template slightly more than twice the diameter of the desired size of the puff, mark and cut the fabric into circles. Turn the 5 mm ($\frac{1}{4}$ in.) seam allowance to the back and, using a double thread, sew around with a running stitch just inside the fold (Diagram 66a). Pull the thread to gather the fabric, leaving a small circular hole in the centre. Knot

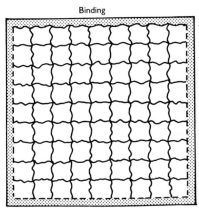

65e A method of attaching lining is to bind the edges together, wrong sides together

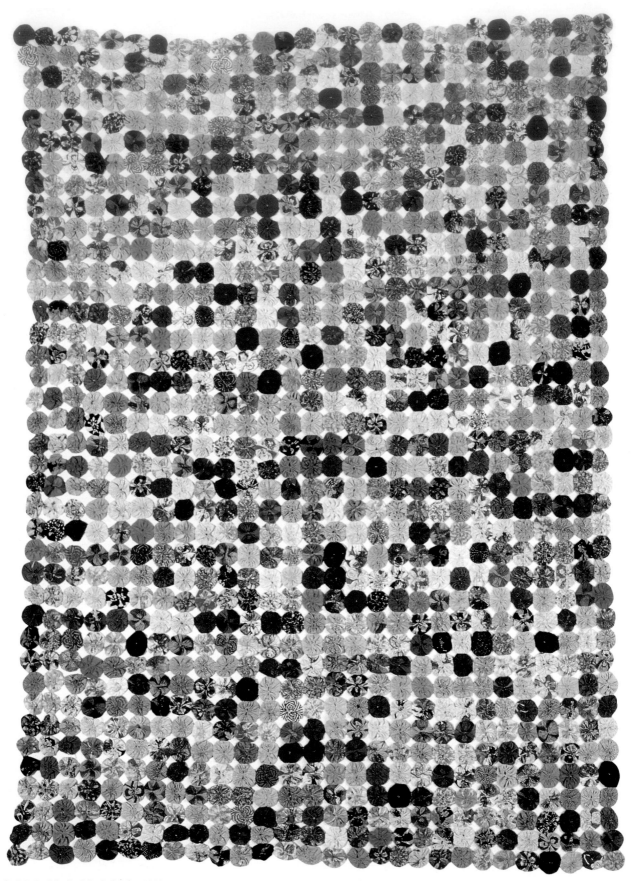

Suffolk Puff Quilt. Made in the 1930s, maker unknown. 183 cm x 168 cm (72 in. x 66 in.). Collection of Jocelyn Campbell

Examples of gathering hand-dyed fabrics into fans and rows by Adèle Outteridge

the thread securely. Press to form a circle with the hole centred (66b).

With right sides together, whipstitch two puffs together along the edge for 5 mm ($\frac{1}{4}$ in.). Then, sew the puffs together in rows (66c). The puffs form their own outer edge and do not require binding.

GATHERING

Working in miniature, Adèle Outteridge has explored the effects of gathering fabric. In her examples, hand-painted fabric has been drawn up on a gathering thread so that only rolls of colour show. The tightness of the gathering determines the width of the roll. In the second example, the fabric has been gathered on one edge only, the other spread out like a fan. The fans are then glued to a backing fabric, mimicking a miniature fan quilt, with the sashes represented by lines of black stitching.

Suffolk Puffs

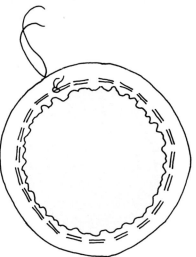

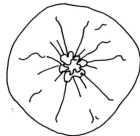

66a Construct a circle template. Cut out circle in fabric. Baste seam allowance with double thread knotted only at beginning

66b Draw up basting thread and knot other end securely

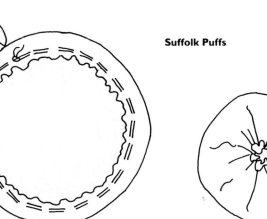

66c Whipstitch puffs together into rows. Then join rows to form quilt top

TUCKING

In her samples, Adèle shows the
variations achieved by changing
the width of the pintuck and the
distance between tucks. Each
width is calculated and the lines
drawn on the right side of the
fabric. The fabric is folded,
pinned along the sewing lines,
and stitched on the right side of
the fabric (see Row 1). The last
two samples in Row 1 show how
the tucks can be pressed to one
side or the other of the stitching
line. In Rows 2 and 3 these
directions are fixed by a line of
sewing anchoring the fold. The
distance between these lines can
be varied.

The example in Row 4 explores
the possibilities of light playing on
a shiny fabric and the effect of
turning part or all of the fold. The
final piece sewn along the cross
grain has rippled, an unexpected
result that is very effective. Row 5
shows the finished product of
these experiments. Adèle has
painted the fabric, tucked it, then
stitched it with gold thread onto
paper she has made herself, which
adds to the texture of the piece.

SLASHING

Inspired by the slashed clothing
of the Crusaders, a technique has
evolved in which stacks of fabric,
sewn together by a grid of
stitching lines, can reveal
glimpses of underlying fabrics
when they are slashed and the top
layers, now in triangles, are
turned back. In this example

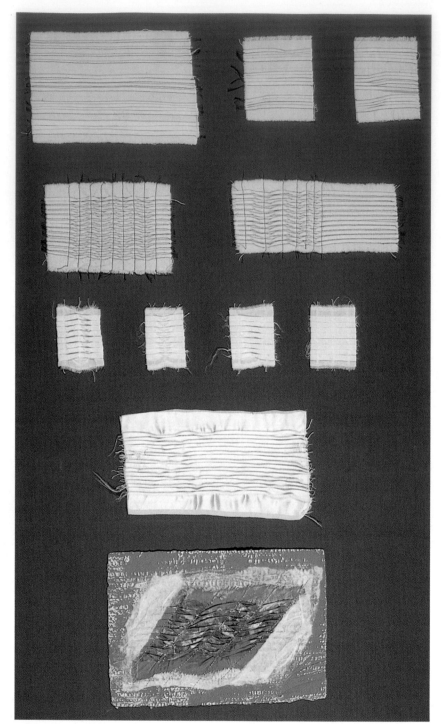

Examples of pintucking fabric on the machine by Adèle Outteridge
From top to bottom:
Row 1 Pressed pintucks
Rows 2 and 3 Pintucks anchored up or down by lines of stitching
Row 4 Variable amounts of the fold being turned
Row 5 The final artwork with tucked, handpainted fabric

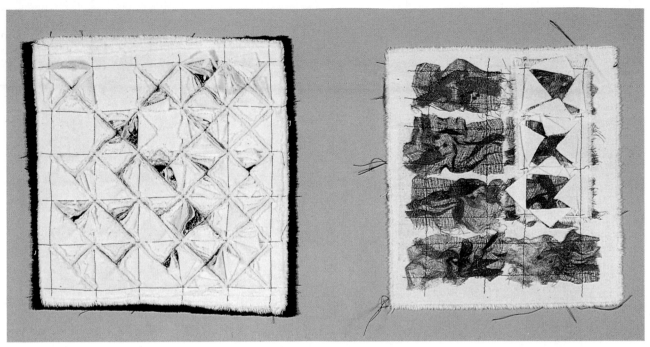

Examples of slashing by Adele Outteridge

Adèle Outteridge has used a plain calico layer, then two calico layers that have a black ripple design screen-printed onto them and, at the bottom, a solid black. Stitched together in a grid of squares, the three top layers are carefully cut from corner to corner in some, but not all, of the squares. The piece was then put through the washing machine and drier several times to fluff out the cut edges. Using pure cotton makes this effect possible. Because she wanted a random effect, only some of the triangles are turned back, to reveal varying amounts of the layers below.

Adéle repeated this exercise using scrunched up, hand-dyed tarlatan that had been secured to the backing layer by red French knots. Only part of this layer was covered by calico before it was all stitched together into a grid. The top calico was slashed to give intriguing glimpses of the tarlatan. She has also substituted acetate and painted paper for a fabric layer in some of her work.

Blue Willow Quilt by Wendy Holland. 216 cm x 168 cm (85 in. x 66 in.). Machine pieced. Hand quilted.

Assembling and Completing the Quilt

Once the quilt top is together, the next step is quilting. The sense of accomplishment that comes with completing one stage and the exciting prospect of making new decisions highlight why quiltmaking is such an absorbing task, as well as breaking up the long process of construction.

The quilting is what distinguishes quilts from other textiles. The quilting line adds another dimension to a quilt, literally and aesthetically. In quilting, all three layers of the work (the top, batting and lining) are finally joined together. They are frequently stretched taut in a hoop or a frame, and then the design is sewn, bringing the layers together with small, even stitches. The line of stitching causes an indentation, creating a three-dimensional effect. Thus the quilt becomes a soft sculpture, its relief determined by the loft of the batting and the degree of quilting. The quilting line can echo the patchwork, emphasising it; it can develop the design theme of the

Bush Garden by Helen Macartney. 237 cm x 225 cm (93 ½ in. x 88 ½ in.). Hand screen-printed. Machine pieced. Hand quilted

top further; or it can be used to create a related or entirely different design, forming an independent element in the overall look of the quilt. The quilting line is a conspicuous and integral part of quilt construction and, as such, good workmanship is an essential goal whether quilting is done by hand or machine.

Finishing the edge of the quilt also requires attention. The edging should complement the style of the patchwork as well as being neat and sturdy. Several types of edges are described here, with reference to illustrations to show the range of possibilities.

Whether they are destined for a wall or a bed, quilts need to be cleaned and repaired over time. So much thought, time and effort goes into making quilts that long-term conservation should be considered. Quilts are not only functional items, but things of beauty and repositories of the memories of the quiltmakers.

QUILTING

DESIGN

The quilting can be designed before the top is sewn or can be worked out in response to the finished top. The significance of the quilting depends on the pattern you choose and its relationship with the patchwork, whether it is on printed or solid fabric, the colour of the thread and the amount of quilting. Many quilts suffer from too little quilting, which is the step that sets quilts apart from other textiles. Large expanses of background fabric can benefit from filler patterns (see examples in Diagram 67) which pack the area down without detracting from more intricate patch work

67 Quilting filler patterns

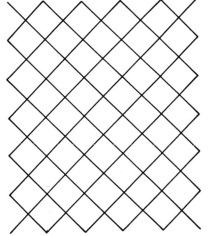

Cross hatching

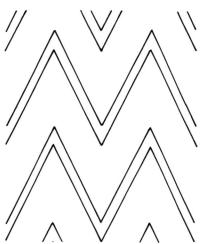

Repeat pattern (double lines)

Clamshells

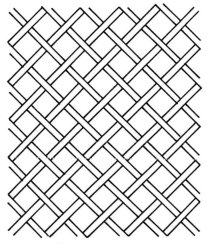

Weave (double lines)

Overlapping circles

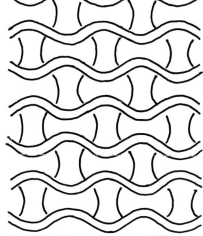

Curved lines (Source: Hornung, 1975)

68 Traditional quilting designs
(Source: Gillon, 1968)

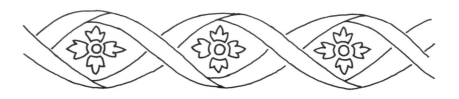

In a wholecloth quilt, where the quilting is the only feature (there being no piecing or appliqué), an overall design is shown to advantage. Marjorie Coleman develops a theme in *Expatriate Shoots* (see page 130). The quilting also becomes a feature in a quilt with large expanses of solid fabric because the quilting line is more obvious than on a print.

In an appliqué quilt the quilting usually outlines the patches. In *Turtles at the Waterhole* (see page 92), Jocelyn Campbell extends the turtle imagery with her double lines of quilting so that the theme is developed over the whole quilt. Often, the background outside the appliqué then looks good packed down with a filler pattern such as cross gridding because the curved quilting lines around the appliqué and the straight gridding in the

background form a pleasing contrast. Other borders can also be created in quilting to provide an interesting feature. Val Moore created a quilted border in *The Flower Press* (see page 94).

Another approach is to repeat the outline of the appliqué with contour quilting. These are lines of quilting running parallel to the edge of the appliqué and at equally spaced distances from it. Sometimes called echo quilting, this technique is common in Hawaiian Appliqué.

The quilting on a pieced top can be approached in many ways. Outline quilting, either in the ditch (along the seam lines) or 5 mm ($\frac{1}{4}$ in.) out, reinforces the lines in the piecing. Using this technique can be more difficult than other forms of quilting because the quilting line constantly changes direction,

requiring repositioning of the hoopful of quilt.

The way in which blocks are joined together may create a secondary design that can be strengthened by quilting. The positioning of light and dark fabrics in the blocks, for example, might suggest a new direction for the quilting. Or you might pick out a motif in the fabric, such as a paisley feature or flower. Margot Child designed a quilted border based on a paisley print that she had used in her quilt, *Morning Star* (see page 43).

Many of the old traditional quilts relied on commercial stencils of feathered wreaths and borders, birds and animals, hearts, flowers and cable patterns. Such patterns are still used today (see Diagram 68 on page 128). New medallion designs can be created by cutting out folded paper as in Hawaiian Appliqué or by designing on a computer (Diagram 69). These are also often flowing, curved designs which complement the straight lines of the piecing, and which can be enlarged or reduced to fit the area available in a particular quilt. Photocopiers make changing the scale easy, or you follow the directions on page 93.

Planning the quilting on the border is very important because it must be designed to turn a corner neatly. The length of the sides is measured and the border patterns can be stretched or compressed slightly if it almost fits. Rather than redesigning the border quilting completely if there is a problem in length, the midpoint of the border is a good place to break the pattern and insert or delete a feature, or to repeat an element of the design to make it the right length. Having worked out the top and bottom, if the border pattern does not fit

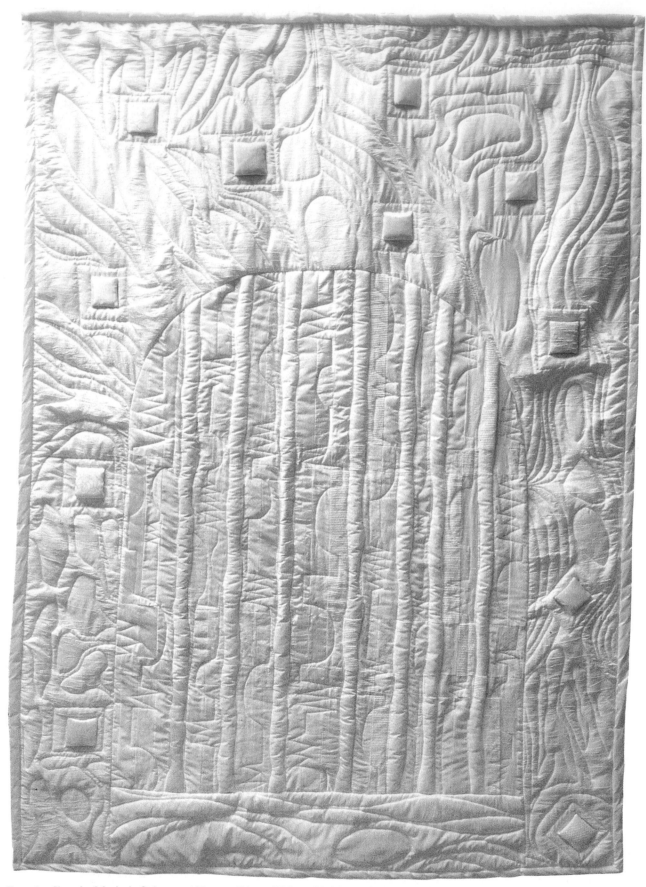

Expatriate Shoots by Marjorie Coleman. 186 cm x 138 cm (73 in. x 54½ in.). Machine pieced and quilted

69 Computer generated quilting designs

Computer designed quilting pattern by Thomas Finnegan, aged 9

Computer designed quilting pattern by Patrick Finnegan, aged 5

evenly along the sides, a different design solution can be found for them.

Many contemporary quilts have an all-over quilting design that does not relate to the construction lines of the patchwork but enhances the design of the total quilt. Trudy Billingsley is one Australian quiltmaker who uses this approach to good effect in *Snorkelling at Beaver Cay* (see page 48). The technique has the advantage of reducing the number of lines to be quilted, and the sweeping lines of quilting are often easier to sew because they do not change direction constantly.

Inspiration for quilting patterns can come from many sources. Other crafts can provide ideas for patterns: stained glass, iron lace, paper cutouts (particularly snowflakes), Celtic designs, Japanese family crests, art nouveau and art deco are but a few of the design sources that can be adapted.

SUPPLIES

FABRIC

When the work is to be handquilted, the weight of the fabric and the thread count (the number of threads to the centimetre or inch in the weave) should be considered. Furnishing fabrics may look wonderful, but they can be hard to needle. A blend often has a higher thread count so here, too, the quilting can be more difficult. Even some pure cottons have this problem — Liberty is one such example. But do not let this deter you if such fabrics are essential to your design, just be aware of their inherent problems and quilt accordingly.

Yvonne Line prefers the effect of handquilting in many of her wall quilts even though fabrics from corduroys through to fine silks may be incorporated in the same work (see page 157). She uses a thicker thread and a much longer stitch to cope with the diversity of fabrics.

Machine quilting can accommodate bulkier and tighter weaves more easily than hand sewing, so you may prefer to use this technique. It's also quicker!

THREAD

For handquilting there are specific quilting threads available. Coats Semco Duet quilting thread is heavier than thread for everyday sewing and is coated in beeswax to make needling easier. The polyester core gives strength while the cotton wrapping makes it compatible with the fabric.

The thread colour may be matched to the fabric or contrasted. The same colour can be used throughout or changed to match each fabric in the top. Ann Haddad's *Southern Skies* on page 132 shows the strong effect of the white quilting thread on a dark blue background. The thread may be further emphasised by using one thicker than normal, such as the crochet thread Wendy Holland sometimes uses. Her stitches are also longer than usual so they stand out.

In machine quilting a normal sewing thread can be used. If you want the stitching to be hidden so that only the indentation of the quilting line is shown, use a colourless nylon thread for the top, with a standard thread in the bobbin. If the top contrasts dramatically in colour to the lining, different coloured threads can be used on the top and the bobbin as long as the tension is balanced so that one colour is not pulled through to the other side.

NEEDLES

Betweens are the easiest needles to use for handquilting. The higher the number of the between, the thinner and shorter the needle and consequently the smaller the stitch. Start with a number 8, and as you become used to it, progress to a 10 and possibly a 12. A problem with the smaller needle is the tiny eye which is harder to thread. It is often a good idea to thread all your needles onto a spool early in the day when the light is good and your eyes are not tired.

When working on the machine, a size 90 (14) needle is preferable because it is less likely to break than a finer needle if it is inadvertently dragged.

BATTING

Medium weight batting is most frequently used. Very thick batts can be used for a comforter that is tied rather than quilted, while very thin batts can be used to create the effect of old and much-loved quilts.

Batts come in several different fibres, and they all have their advantages and problems. The most common problem is fibre migration or bearding. Individual fibres that make up the batt can

Southern Skies by Ann Haddad. 192 cm x 160 cm (75½ in. x 63 in.). Hand and machine pieced. Hand quilted

work their way through the quilt top and lining. This bearding is particularly obvious on dark fabrics, and not only looks unsightly, but means that over time the batt thins out as fibres are lost.

Various treatments attempt to prevent this migration. Bonded batts have a surface glaze that should reduce the movement of the fibres. Bonded batts come in polyester, poly-cotton blends, pure cotton and pure wool. Some polyester batts are needle punched so that all the fibres are interlocked and less likely to beard.

Polyester batts are the most common: they have a high loft

and wash well. The flatter effect achieved by quilting through pure cotton batts is reminiscent of old quilts, and is preferred by some quiltmakers for that reason. However, the cotton tends to break up with washing unless it is very heavily quilted (about 2.5 cm or 1 in. apart).

The poly-cotton blend allows a wide spacing of quilting while retaining the low loft and density of a polyester batt. Like the all-cotton batt, it shrinks with washing, so should be prewashed.

Pure wool batts drape well and are light and warm. They also retain their loft well. However, some of the earlier versions bearded very badly. Also,

Pinmill by Wendy Holland. 203 cm x 183 cm (80 in. x 72 in.). Machine pieced. Hand quilted

washing them requires great care or they could shrink.

The loft of the batt is another consideration. Obviously the thinner the batt, the smaller the quilting stitches. Wall quilts should lie flat, so a stiffer batt is more appropriate, whereas a bed quilt looks better draped.

SAFETY PINS

Small, rustproof pins can be used for basting.

FRAMES

The slightly puckered effect of handquilting is best realised by stretching the work in a frame while quilting. When the tension is released, the quilting line indents slightly.

The type of frame you choose depends on the way you prefer to work. A frame the full width of the quilt gives an even tension and shows a large area of the quilt at any one time. Its disadvantages are the space it takes up, lack of portability and its fixed nature which does not allow the work to be turned. This means that the quilting lines may have to be sewn in what is not always the most comfortable direction, but the awkwardness is easily overcome with practice.

A hoop is a popular choice. A circular one gives an even tension so, although an oval one holds more of the quilt top, tensioning it is more difficult. Choose the size best suited to your work and your comfort. Too small and the hoop does not contain much of the quilt, which has to be moved frequently; too large and the hand underneath cannot comfortably reach the needle. Depending on the length of the quilter's arm, a hoop of 40 cm (16 in.) to 60 cm (24 in.) is appropriate.

A rectangular or square plastic tubular frame allows the quilter to

sew into the corners of a block. The size and shape can be changed according to the lengths chosen to make up the frame, so it can be tailored to fit a particular border or block. By merely twisting the casing that holds the quilt to each arm of the frame underneath, a very tight and even tension can be achieved.

THIMBLES

A thimble to fit the middle finger of the sewing hand is essential to push the needle back up through the layers to complete the quilting stitch.

A metal thimble with indentations for the needle to lodge in works well. Some have a raised end which aids quilting; a few have no end at all, to accommodate sewers with long fingernails. Silver thimbles are beautiful, but be sure they are properly indented. If buying an old one, make sure that holes have not been worn through the indentations by a previous owner.

Leather thimbles appeal to some because of their greater flexibility. Keep them away from the dog, who will love to chew on them!

PREPARING THE LINING OR BACKING FABRIC

Like all the fabric in the top, the lining needs to be washed, ironed, and the selvedges removed. Depending on the size of the top, the lining may need to be seamed together. If you are trying to conserve fabric use a central seam (Diagram 70a), but if possible avoid one because handquilting becomes less even through extra layers of seam allowance (70b and c). Some quilters make a feature

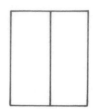

70a Lengths joined with central seam

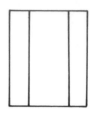

70b Lengths joined avoiding central seam

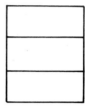

70c Lengths joined across quilt avoiding central seam

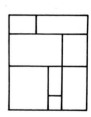

70d Patched lining

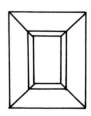

70e Reversible quilt

of the back, putting together several fabrics so that the quilt is reversible (70d and e). This is a good way of using up fabrics.

MARKERS

There is a lot of controversy about which marker should be used to transfer the quilting design to the fabric. If they have never been washed old quilts still often show the original pencil lines. Although the mark is still visible, it was a reliable method and some quilters use it today. Prue Socha recommends other methods which include silver pencils which show up well on dark fabrics, or chalk which can be used for small sections, although it rubs off quickly. Water soluble pens leave no visible trace, and the ones that disappear quickly encourage you to work fast! The long-term effect of these pens, however, is uncertain: sometimes the marks reappear — permanently!

For marking grids and other straight lines, masking tape is useful except that it cannot be left on the quilt for prolonged periods because the glue comes off on the fabric.

BASTING

To prevent one layer of fabric slipping away from another, something that causes puckers in the quilting, the top, batting and lining should be securely basted together. Before basting, check that all the loose threads on the top are clipped and that any dark seam allowances are not showing through lighter fabrics. Immediately before basting, press the top and lining so that no creases are incorporated.

If you have the room it is best to stretch out the whole quilt ready for basting, as if it is in a

frame. Doing this also prevents puckers in the quilting. Wrong side up, pin the lining into the carpet, starting in the centre of opposite sides and working out to the corners. Repeat for the two remaining sides. If two people work together on opposite sides, a good tension can be maintained. If your carpet is not big enough, a friend's house or a nearby church or community hall may have a large enough expanse. It is definitely a community activity, because the more helpers, the quicker it gets done!

Place the batting on top of the lining, smoothing out any wrinkles. If it needs to be seamed, abut the pieces and, using white thread, take large stitches, drawing the sides together. Stitch it as if you were lacing up a shoe, or use a herringbone stitch.

Centre the top over the lining, making sure that the seam lines all line up. This is particularly important if the lining is a striped fabric, otherwise the quilting lines will not align with the stripes. Stretch the top and pin into the carpet as you did with the lining.

Quilts are traditionally basted with long stitches. Baste from the centre out, first the quarters, then the diagonals out to the corners, and then halving the distance between these lines. Continue to fill in the spaces with lines of basting radiating from the centre until there is no area greater than a fist width unbasted (Diagram 71a).

Thread basting can be a hindrance in machine quilting. The stitching happens so quickly that it is inconvenient to stop constantly to cut the basting threads before they are stitched over, which would make them harder to remove. Small, rustproof safety pins anchor the layers effectively and can be

Basting the quilt

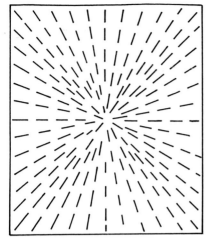

71a Thread baste quilt in radial pattern

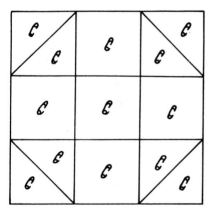

71b Pin baste avoiding quilting lines

spaced to avoid lines of quilting. Place them at intervals of about 15 cm (6 in.) (Diagram 71b).

TRANSFERRING THE DESIGN

If the quilting pattern is independent of the patchwork, the design needs to be drawn onto the top. For an all-over pattern this is best done before the quilt is basted. For smaller sections it is possible to transfer the design as you quilt.

If the pattern is drawn on the top before basting, the pattern can be placed under the fabric and over a light source which will make the markings show through easily. Tape it to the window or a light-table (see page 103), or you can use an overhead projector if you have access to one.

To transfer a complicated design to a basted quilt, tape stiff netting (used for bridal veils) over the design and draw over the lines with a soft pencil. Then pin the netting onto the quilt and trace over the lines. When the netting is removed, the dashed lines on the fabric preserve the pattern. Silver pencil, chalk (which can rub off easily) or soapstone will show up on dark fabrics.

The pattern can also be transferred by stencil. You can either use a commercial one or you can design one of your own. In the latter case, if the design is complicated, all the intersections would make the stencil fall apart. Instead, break it up into several sections with different parts of the design on each, and then trace to build up the design.

HAND QUILTING

Thread the needle and knot the thread using the technique described on page 72.

Always start handquilting in the centre of the quilt and work out towards the sides. This way if any folds have been basted in, the basting can be released and the excess smoothed out. Place the quilt in a frame or hoop and stretch it to an even tension.

Pop the knot right through the top and into the batting by giving it a quick tug. Sew through all three layers with a running stitch. The stitch is made with a rocking motion: with the needle lodged in the thimble on the middle finger of the hand, it is pushed down through the quilt until it touches

Heirloom of Wildflowers (detail) by Kerry Gavin. 280 cm x 210 cm (110 in. x 82½ in.). Hand quilted wholecloth quilt with backstitched wildflowers in embroidery thread

the finger or thimble of the other hand underneath. This finger then forces the needle up so that the smallest possible stitch is taken.

One stitch at a time can be taken or several stitches can be loaded onto the needle before it is pulled through. If the needle sticks a little in the fabric, run the needle through your hair or stab it into some soap or a pincushion filled with wool fleece to grease it slightly. If it really sticks, use a

rubber glove or balloon to grasp it and pull it out.

To begin with, the quilting stitch can feel strange and could take some practice before it feels comfortable. Concentrate first on making the stitches an even length, in time they will get smaller. Small, evenly spaced stitches are the common goal, unless a particular effect is required. In a bed quilt the stitch should not be so long that you could catch a nail in it.

The running stitch is the most popular stitch for quilting but there are occasions when other stitches are appropriate. Kerry Gavin used a backstitch in different coloured threads to highlight the flowers in her *Heirloom of Wildflowers*, while Prue Socha couched her running stitch with an embroidery thread of a different colour in *Japanese Hillside* (see page 17).

Sometimes there is a lot of thread left on the needle when a line of quilting is finished. If the closest line is more than the length of the needle away, push the needle into the batting towards the desired spot. Further on, bring up the point and, holding it half out of the quilt, rotate the needle eye towards the next spot. Bring up the needle eye halfway out of the fabric and this time rotate the point. Repeat this until the thread has travelled through the batting to the next line of quilting. Obviously it is not worth travelling too far or all the thread will be taken up.

To finish off a thread, do a backstitch and then make a knot in the thread near the fabric surface. Pierce the last stitch with the needle and pop the knot through it down into the batting. Bring the needle up some distance away and snip the thread. This way the tag (the end of the thread) will not work free.

Try never to bleed on the quilt! If you do prick your finger, use saliva on a piece of fabric to rub away the blood.

MACHINE QUILTING

Machine quilting is suited to long, unbroken lines. Some machines handle the thickness of three

Greg Somerville machine quilting. The quilt is rolled to allow it to pass under the head of the sewing machine

layers better than others, so refer to your sewing machine manual for guidance. Loosening the upper tension may help, and a quilting (walking) foot or darning foot might be of assistance. Use stitch length 4 to contend with the extra thickness and sew slowly, smoothing the work to prevent puckers. Slightly stretch the work by holding it on either side of the needle. If the work bunches up, place your hands in front of and behind the needle and pull slightly; this will help ease the fabric under the needle. This is useful when two lines of quilting cross.

To avoid having one unsightly tuck, if a pucker is unavoidable, leave the needle in the fabric, then, raising the presser foot, use your seam ripper to guide a little extra fabric under the needle. Put down the presser foot and turn the hand wheel to make one stitch. Repeat this several times and the pucker will be distributed less obviously over a greater length.

To turn corners, leave the needle in the work, lift the presser foot, rotate the quilt and lower the presser foot before sewing.

There are several ways of securing the threads at the start and finish of each line of stitching. One option is to draw the top thread to the back, tie it with the other thread in a reef knot, thread the ends in a needle and bury the threads in the batting. A quicker but slightly more visible solution is achieved by reducing the stitch length to nearly zero at the beginning and end of a line so that the stitches almost pile up and interlock themselves. Just snip the threads at the surface. If straight lines of stitching run from one edge of the quilt to the other, they do not need to be secured because they will be locked into place by the stitching of the binding.

The problem with machine quilting is the huge bulk of fabric that needs to pass under the head of the machine. Roll the quilt up tightly so that it fits through the arch of the machine more easily. If the quilting line changes direction, you may need to roll and unroll the quilt while it is under the needle. This can be difficult. Keep the needle in the work and the presser foot up while repositioning the quilt, and always smooth the work out before resuming stitching.

The weight of the quilt can also cause drag, so try to work with a table on your left which can hold the bulk of the quilt.

Free machine quilting overcomes this problem as the stitching can follow any direction. Loops are as easy as straight lines because the quilt does not have to be rotated. *Terra Australis* is heavily quilted in this manner to give the impression of weathering patterns in the rock strata, and took only a couple of weeks to finish (see page 34).

Free machine quilting gives enormous freedom. The needle can be used as a pencil to scribble on a design. To do this, drop the machine's feed dog, reduce the stitch length to zero and raise the height of the presser foot so that it glides over the top of the fabric with little friction. The presser foot lever must be dropped to engage the tension. A darning foot may help. Run the machine fast so that the needle clears the fabric often, otherwise it may break as you pull the quilt against it. An even stitch length will come with practice.

All machine quilting should be practised on scrap materials before sewing the quilt. Use the same weight fabric and batting as the finished work while practising so that the adjustments suit the quilt.

CORDING AND TRAPUNTO

A double line of quilting always looks handsome and cording can enhance this effect. The cord is threaded along the channel between the two quilting lines.

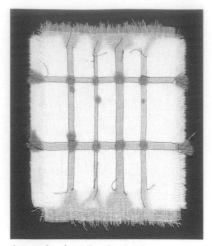

A sample of cording by Adèle Outteridge, showing the back of the work

The height of important areas of a quilt pattern can be further elevated by stuffing extra batting behind them. This is called trapunto. Marjorie Coleman has used trapunto in *Expatriate Shoots* (see page 130). Both cording and trapunto require an extra layer of fabric as a foundation.

Choose a fine fabric for handquilting. If it has a slightly open weave, such as cheesecloth, the threads can be separated to introduce the cord or batting, rather than cutting it open and resewing it.

For cording, the parallel lines of quilting keeping the top and the foundation fabric together and providing the channel for the cord, should be smooth and flowing. A running stitch or a backstitch can be used for this quilting.

Using a bodkin and a thick cotton, wool or acrylic cord, insert the bodkin into the channel from the back and travel the cord along it for about 5 cm (2 in.) before emerging. Leaving a little loop of spare cord, re-enter the channel in exactly the same spot and run in the same direction. If lines of cording cross, work out which one lies underneath in the design and bring this cord out of the fabric at the back, then re-enter on the

other side of the top cord. Continue leaving small loops at intervals: they will be taken up over time, and will prevent the cord from pulling.

To raise some areas of the pattern with trapunto, stitch around the outline to form an enclosed space. Separate the threads of the foundation fabric, or slit it and insert some batting. For precision it can be wound onto the end of a toothpick. Fill up the corners first and then work towards the centre. Do not overstuff the area or it will look tight and strained. Repair any slits.

When the cording and/or trapunto is finished, baste the top, batting and lining in the usual manner and then quilt further. The trapunto, for example, can be complemented by *stipple quilting*. In stipple quilting areas of the quilt are packed down by quilting lines made so close together (about 3 mm or $\frac{1}{8}$ in.) that they lose their individual impact and have a textural effect as well as compacting the quilt, leaving the trapunto in high relief.

SHADOW APPLIQUÉ QUILTING

A shadow or veiled effect can be achieved by overlaying an appliquéd top with a fine organza, then quilting through this layer to secure the appliqué in place. The edges of the appliqué do not have to be turned under because the quilting line secures it to the quilt top. Lorna Firth has used this effect to advantage in her quilt, *Flower Shadows*. The colours in the appliqué are muted by the sheer overlay, resulting in a very soft effect.

Flower Shadows by Lorna Firth. 196 cm x 163 cm (77 in. x 64 in.). Shadow appliqué with hand embroidered details. Hand appliquéd and quilted

TYING

There are times when quilting is inappropriate and tying is the best option. The quilt might be too thick, or lack of time could be a problem. Log Cabin quilts, for example, with their thick foundation fabrics and close seam allowances were often tied in the past. Quilts can be tied in just a few hours. The knots can be

Tying a quilt

72a Starting from the side the tails are to show, pass needle down through layers and back up again

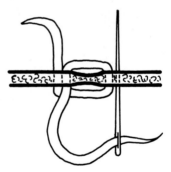

72b Pull tight and repeat

72c Tie ends in reef knot. Cut ends evenly

distributed evenly as part of the pattern, or they can be made randomly. They should be spaced at least every 18 cm (8 in.).

First, baste the layers securely, as for quilting. Then, choose a thread, which may be acrylic or wool, double it, and make a knot. The thread is visible, so make a feature of it by using a thicker thread than usual. The tails of the knot can show on the top or the bottom, or they can be threaded into the batting. Starting with the side where the tails will show, pass the needle down through the material and up again (Diagram 72a). Repeat (72b). Tie with a reef knot, left over right, right over left (72c). Snip the ends evenly, leaving tails of about 2 cm ($\frac{3}{4}$ in.), unless they are to be buried in the quilt. Marli Popple tied red ribbons to great effect in *Broulee* (see page 38).

FINISHING

EDGES

When the quilting is complete the edges have to be finished. The quilts opposite show a variety of finishes, from a bound edge to a sawtooth edge.

SELF FINISHES

One finish can even precede quilting: right sides together, the top, lining, and perhaps the batt, are sewn almost all the way around the edges. The excess of the batt is trimmed back to the stitching line and the corners trimmed before the quilt is pulled right side out through the opening, which is then slipstitched, whipstitched, machine stitched or handquilted

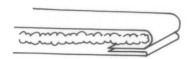

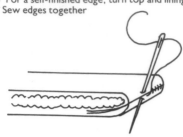

73 For a self-finished edge, turn top and lining in. Sew edges together

close to the edge (Diagram 73). This pillowcase effect can also be achieved after quilting. A lining can be attached as long as the quilting lines do not come too close to the edge where they could be hidden in the seam allowance. The batt is trimmed back to the stitching line, the edges of the top and lining straightened and the top seam allowances tucked over the batt, enclosing it. The edge is finished as above.

ONE SIDE FOLDED OVER THE OTHER

Sometimes, to finish a quilt, the top is folded over to the back (Diagram 74a) or the lining brought over to the front (74b). A seam allowance is then turned under and the edge hand appliquéd or machined in place. Finishing by this method gives the appearance of a binding without

One side folded over the other

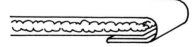

74a Either fold quilt top over lining and sew **or**

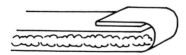

74b Fold lining over quilt top and sew

Finishes for quilts (from top to bottom): wide binding and cut-off corners for *Basket Quilt,* turned-in edges for *Japanese Hillside,* narrow binding for *Lollipop Lane,* scallops and rounded corners for *Yellow Drunkard's Path,* prairie points for *The Flower Press,* hexagons forming an irregular edge for *Search for School Grey*

Separate Binding

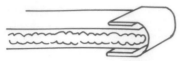

75a Separate binding can be made either of the same or contrasting fabric to the quilt top.

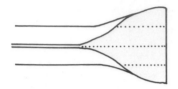

75b Cut fabric four times the width of finished binding. Fold strip in half then turn each edge in to meet at central crease.

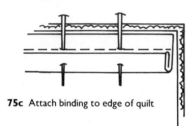

75c Attach binding to edge of quilt

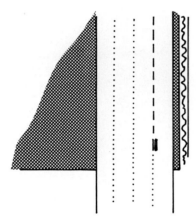

75d To mitre the binding, stitch it to quilt edge. Stop near corner at intersection of seam lines

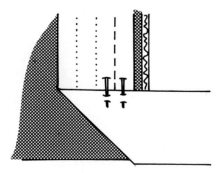

75e Fold binding to right side at 45° angle to quilt edge. Press fold line. Pin in place

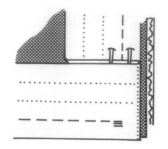

75f Fold binding back from quilt edge. Align edge of binding with next quilt edge to be sewn. Stitch out from intersection of seam lines along the quilt edge

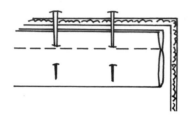

75g For double binding align edges of binding with quilt. Pin and stitch in one-third of the distance from the edges.

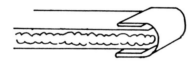

75h Turn binding over to other edge of top and hand appliqué down.

the extra work. However, it is not as strong, and will not lie as flat if the quilt is hung.

SEPARATE BINDING

More commonly, the edge is enclosed in a binding, which can be made of a contrasting fabric or can match the top or the lining (Diagram 75a). Because it has to hold a crease, the binding is best cut from pure cotton. It is usually quite narrow, about 1 cm ($\frac{1}{2}$ in.) when finished. The binding can be cut on the straight or the cross. The latter has more give, and must be used if the edge is curved. Depending on how it is sewn, it should be four or six times the finished width.

The most common method of making binding is to cut it on the cross four times the finished width, then, with wrong sides together, press the binding in half. Each edge of the binding is then turned in to the crease and pressed again. This creates bias binding (75b).

To attach it to the quilt, open it out and, with the right sides of the quilt and binding together and edges aligned, sew along the crease (75c). Mitre the corners if they are at right angles. When approaching a corner, sew exactly to the intersection of the sewing lines and backstitch to secure the thread (75d). Fold the binding to the right side away from the quilt on a 45° diagonal (75e). Press the fold. Pin the edge of the binding to the corner of the quilt and fold the binding back so the fold line exactly lines up with the wrong side of the quilt. The edge of the binding is aligned with the next edge of the quilt to be bound. Rotate the quilt by 90° and start sewing the binding to the quilt along this edge, beginning at the pressed diagonal fold line (75f). When the binding is turned to the other side, sew to the intersection of the sewing lines, then tuck under some binding to form a mitre, before sewing out along the next side. Hand appliqué the diagonals in place.

Sometimes the corners are rounded, in which case the binding must be eased around the curve. Fold the binding over to the back and hand appliqué the binding in place, just covering the last line of stitching.

Another method is to cut the binding six times the finished width to create a double binding which is stronger. With wrong sides together, press the binding in half. Right sides together, align both the edges of the binding and

Continuous bias

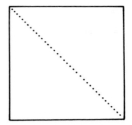

76a Take a square of fabric and cut along diagonal

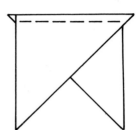

76b Sew triangles together, right sides facing

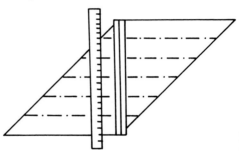

76c Press seam allowances open. Mark parallel cutting lines

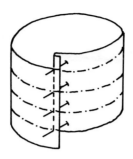

76d Offset lines by one row, match opposing cutting lines, leaving seam allowance. Pin and sew

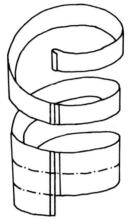

76e On newly formed cylinder cut along marked lines to form continuous bias tape

edges, ensuring that you sew in a straight line through the pinned spots. Press the seams open. Begin cutting the bias length from the top of the tube, following the marked cutting lines (76e).

PRAIRIE POINT EDGE OR SAWTOOTH

Sometimes a serrated edge can enhance a quilt. There are several ways of folding the triangles that make up the Prairie Points. Fold small squares diagonally in half (Diagrams 77a and b). Press. Fold in half on the diagonal again (77c). These newly formed triangles are then pinned to the right side of the edge to be bound,

Prairie Point from a diagonal fold

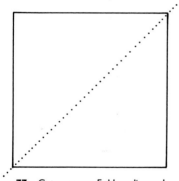

77a Cut a square. Fold on diagonal

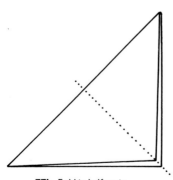

77b Fold in half again

77c Finished Prairie Point

the quilt, then stitch just under one-third of the width of the binding out from the quilt edge (75g). Mitre the corners. Turn the binding over to the back and hand appliqué the finished edge (75h). In this case, a seam allowance does not need to be turned under because the edge is a fold, not a raw edge.

If there are inner corners (as in the quilt pictured), these should be mitred.

CONTINUOUS BINDING

Rather than cutting individual strips at an angle of 45° to the grain, you can make continuous binding.

Start with a 115 cm (45 in.) square of fabric. Fold it in half to make a triangle and press fold lightly to find the bias line (Diagram 76a). Cut the fabric apart along this line. With rights sides together, machine the two triangles together along the straight edge (76b), with a 5 mm ($\frac{1}{4}$ in.) seam allowance. Press the seam open. On the wrong side of the fabric, mark cutting lines the desired distance apart (this will be the width of the binding), making sure that the lines are parallel (76c). Right sides together, drop the lines on one side by one row so that they are offset. Pin through these lines, 5 mm ($\frac{1}{4}$ in.) in (76d). Join the two

Prairie Point from a horizontal fold

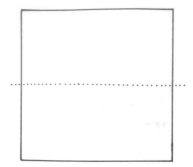

78a Cut a square and fold in half along horizontal

78b Finger press quarter lines

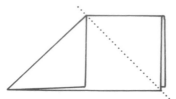

78c Fold down one corner to quarter line crease

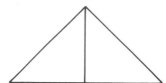

78d Fold other corner down to form finished Prairie Point

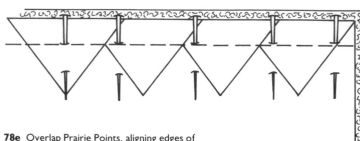

78e Overlap Prairie Points, aligning edges of points with quilt top. Pin and sew.

edges aligned. By beginning to pin the triangles a short distance in from the corner, that corner will appear to be one of the points. Distribute the points uniformly along the edge to finish the same distance in from the next corner. They can be overlapped, so long as the overlapping is maintained evenly. Sew the points to the quilt top. Turn the seam allowance in so the Prairie Points show, then place the lining on top of this and sew a 5 mm ($\frac{1}{4}$ in.) seam almost around the quilt. Turn right sides out and press. Whipstitch or slipstitch the opening.

A different effect results from another system of folds. Cut small squares and fold in half (Diagram 78a), then finger press them into quarters to give the crease line (78b). Lift back the corners so the original square is once again folded in half. Take each corner of the fold and pull it down to the crease line (78c). Press in place (78d). The points are overlapped and sewn as before.

HEXAGONS

Quilts like Nancy Tingey's *Search for School Grey* (see page 12) are edged in hexagons. If the hexagons are not appliquéd onto a backing fabric, they can be backed with another hexagon so that the edge formed follows the sides and points of the hexagons that make up the quilt. Nancy Tingey uses this effect and sometimes plays on it by making the outside row of hexagons discontinuous, so that the edge seems organic and more like a natural object than if a straight line had been used. Each outside hexagon is backed by another and whipstitched in place. This

backing hexagon is then appliquéd onto the lining (Diagram 79).

SIGNING THE QUILT

After all the care and thought that goes into a quilt, it should be signed and dated on completion. Quilt historians of the future will appreciate the information, and friends and viewers in the present will enjoy the personal touch. Some people sign their quilts on the back, either on a separate piece of fabric or directly onto the lining. A permanent marker can

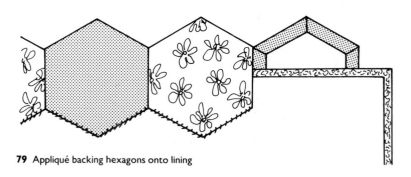

79 Appliqué backing hexagons onto lining

be used to write details on a solid fabric. This is then heat-set with an iron and hand appliquéd to a bottom corner of the back. For exhibition organisers information such as the quilt name, maker, dimensions and date are useful.

Wendy Holland designs a signature incorporating her initials and the year and silkscreens copies for each quilt she makes that year. The signature itself becomes a work of art.

Quilts can also be signed on the front or back using embroidery stitches. Several stitches can be used, but backstitch or a chain stitch are the most popular. Use an embroidery thread in a contrasting colour so that it shows up.

The signature can also be quilted into the design of the quilt top. On the Double Wreath block of a sampler quilt that I made for my parents-in-law I included the initials of family members and the date.

CARE OF QUILTS

HANGING

To display a quilt on a wall, sew a sleeve along the top of the back that will accommodate a flat length of timber. Suspend the timber between cuphooks on the wall. If the quilt is very wide and the fabric heavy, the sleeve may need to be constructed in sections so that the length of timber it holds can be supported by several hooks along its length.

Quilts can also be stretched or velcroed over a frame for wall display, such as the *Hunters Hill*

Double Wreath block by Dianne Finnegan. 38 cm x 38 cm (15 in. x 15 in.). Hand pieced and quilted

Bicentennial Quilt (see page 150). Sleeves stitched to the back of the quilt on all sides can accommodate a frame. Insert each length of timber or plastic tubing into the sleeves, then fasten the corners of the frame. If velcro is to be used, attach the second strip of velcro to a frame of timber that will be fixed on the wall.

Hang the quilt in a place where it is not exposed to direct sunlight and where it is unlikely to be touched. It is possible to protect any edges that are within reach by mounting a sheet of perspex that does not touch the fabric, to act as a shield.

STORAGE

Folding and storing quilts in a cupboard for long periods can result in strong crease lines. And if they are in contact with wood they may stain. The quilts should be wrapped in acid-free tissue paper, and refolded every now and then along different crease lines. If there is any wool in the quilt remember to take measures to protect it from moths. Never store quilts in plastic garbage bags, even for a short time — there have been too many cases where someone has inadvertently thrown them out! Quilts should not be stored in plastic bags for long periods anyway, because the moisture in the quilt may cause mildew.

Quilts are better stored if they are rolled right side out and wrapped in a sheet. The best place for a quilt that is being stored is on a bed, perhaps in a guest room. If cats and children are likely to climb on the bed, cover the quilt.

Pale Ladies by Wendy Holland. 240 cm x 198 cm (94½ in. x 78 in.). Machine pieced. Hand quilted

CLEANING

If you have made the quilt yourself you will know that the fabrics have been prewashed and are colour fast. Otherwise, you should test the fabrics for bleeding. Strong reds, purples and blues are the colours most likely to run. Test them by wetting a piece of white or cream fabric and rubbing it on each colour to see if any colour comes off. If a fabric does lose some colour, it may be best to spot clean the quilt, shake it or gently vacuum it. Dry cleaning is an option if you have a very good dry cleaner. However, I have heard horror stories of uneven shrinkage that has ruined quilts that have gone through the dry cleaning process.

Although they may be hung out of range of prying fingers, wall quilts do collect dust and need to be shaken and vacuumed once or twice a year. Place a stocking over the nozzle of the vacuum cleaner to reduce the suction and protect the fabric.

Quilts made from washable fabrics can be washed by hand or by machine. Use a wool mix washing detergent and cold or warm water.

If you are going to wash your quilts by hand it is best, because of their size, to wash them in the bath. Removing all the dirt and detergent is important, so rinse the quilt several times. Gently squeeze out the excess water and hang over a couple of lines to dry. Change the position of the quilt several times while it dries to prevent creasing. Choose a windy day to speed drying, and if possible dry the quilt out of strong sunlight.

If you choose to machine wash, use a gentle cycle and remove the quilt as soon as the cycle has finished. It may be put through the dryer on the warm setting, although quilts with wool batts could shrink and should not go in the dryer.

Old quilts may be fragile and could tear if subjected to normal washing. If in doubt, contact the conservator at your local museum and ask for advice.

CONSERVING

Relatively new quilts that have been torn may be repaired by carefully unpicking the torn patches and sewing in replacements, matching the fabrics as closely as possible. The binding nearest the head of a bed is often the first part of a quilt to show wear. The quilt can be rebound, either by removing the frayed binding and sewing on a new one, or by sewing a new binding over the old one.

Old quilts should be conserved rather than repaired. Ask at a museum for advice about where to buy sheer fabric that can be basted over the worn spot to protect it from further disintegration.

A cupboard full of quilts. The carving on the cupboard suggests a quilting pattern

Finishing Touches

Practically, a finished quilt can be used for all sorts of purposes, but the intangible use of a quilt is harder to quantify. The enjoyment of making it, the memories incorporated in it (both in the fabrics used as well as the life experiences passed through during its construction), and the creative purpose expressed in it, all become woven into the quilt's fabric.

The actual making of a quilt can be as important to a quiltmaker as the finished product. While many quiltmakers for the most part work alone, it is a part of the quiltmaking tradition that quiltmakers frequently meet regularly with others to sew. Stemming from the earliest days of the craft, quiltmaking remains a communal activity. Because quilts may be very large and because they often take so long to make, they lend themselves to community participation. The construction of group quilts can draw people together by providing a common purpose. Group quilts can be made for many reasons: in commemoration of important events, for community use, or to celebrate friendship. The following accounts look at a range of community projects and how they came into being.

This final section of *Piece By Piece* also incorporates a glossary of terms, diagrams of some traditional block patterns and illustrations of some of the more frequently used embroidery stitches.

GROUP QUILTS

Quilts are a wonderful medium for expressing love or to commemorate events. Quilts to be made for hanging in public places, as raffle quilts to raise money, as charity quilts, perhaps for use on hospital beds, as gifts for people to mark a special occasion or just as a token of friendship, can unite a community in a common purpose. The stories behind the following quilts provide an interesting social history as well as giving practical advice on how to coordinate group quilts.

THE HUNTERS HILL BICENTENNIAL QUILT

An account by Alysoun Ryves, President of the Hunters Hill Quilters:
Australia's Bicentenary in 1988 prompted many communities to celebrate by making a quilted wall-hanging depicting the local

area. In 1982 Joanne Gordon suggested a quilt be made in response to a request from the Hunters Hill Bicentennial Committee for projects to involve local residents. The Hunters Hill Quilters were grateful to receive financial assistance for the project from the Hunters Hill Council, which was made possible by a grant from the New South Wales Bicentennial Council.

The geography of the area (Hunters Hill is on a peninsula) gave Margot Child the inspiration for the form of the quilt, a pictorial map (with a lot of artistic licence!). Trudy Billingsley gave us valuable advice when we began. Judy Burgess made more of the quilt than anyone else. Her artist's training, combined with her vast experience in quilting, shows in her beautiful, detailed work, and made her (by default) the artistic director: "Do it again, it's too small" and "Don't worry, I'll fix that later"

In early 1986 several groups were organised. The "material group" collected fabrics from wherever they could be found. At the same time the "drawing

Hunters Hill Bicentennial Quilt by members of the Hunters Hill Quilters. 250 cm x 500 cm (98½ in. x 197 in.). Machine pieced. Hand and machine appliquéd. Hand embroidered. Hand quilted

group" scaled up the map, coloured it and made templates in blocks 50 cm square. The fabric was cut, sewn together, pressed, rearranged, changed (who suggested that velvet?) and resewn. The background was finished in August of that year.

The "sewing group" involved more than 50 people, making appliquéd houses, churches, trees, boats, more trees, windsurfers, even an airship, and still more trees. We sewed the pieces on (mostly in the right places on the map) and, amazingly, all the buildings depicted, except two, are real ones, and some are even recognisable! Many of us made our own houses, so there is a diverse mix of period and styles in the buildings shown, as well as variety and character in the sewing.

In January 1988 Judy Burgess sewed on the borders, then in February we began quilting, first around the appliqué, then the background. Dianne Finnegan drew the quilting lines for us: waves in the Parramatta and Lane Cove Rivers, contour lines on the land and lovely swirls of wind in the sky. The quilting was fun, with up to eight of us at a time sitting around the big borrowed quilting frame, chatting and drinking lots of coffee. Most of the quilting was finished one March afternoon, in spite of a terrific thunderstorm which seemed to electrify our needles.

The quilt was removed from the frame and then the border was turned under. We spent most of May telling ourselves it was all done even though we were still making numerous finishing touches. A couple more houses appeared at this stage, too, and we moved a tree or two to fit them. in.

Two men played important

parts in the project. Marsh Burgess altered the quilting frame to suit us and Carl Ryves made the mount so the quilt could be hung. Unfortunately, we could not persuade them to sew, or even to make the coffee, but they helped to drink it, and enjoyed socialising with the ladies.

For those who are interested in statistics, the quilt measures 6 m (18 ft) by 2.5 m ($7\frac{1}{2}$ ft) and took almost 3000 man, no, sorry, woman hours to make, with 57 women taking part, in just over two years. There are 66 buildings, 71 boats and windsurfers, 13 clubs and badges, three monuments, one bridge, and you can count the trees yourself! The whole thing was finished on the morning of the presentation, but the embroidered signatures took a little longer.

Our quilt was presented to Hunters Hill Council on 26 May 1988. Then came the fun for the Council engineers! They had to carry the quilt on its frame from the stage door around the outside to the front of the Town Hall, then remove the front doors to get the quilt into the foyer! Now it hangs opposite the entrance and we believe it is a testimony to the friendship of all who took part in making it — and is also perhaps a guide to Hunters Hill!

THE QUILTERS' GUILD SIGNATURE QUILT

An account by Dianne Finnegan, Past President of The Quilters' Guild:

To raise money for Quilt Australia, a major national exhibition, Andrea O'Halloran suggested that we should make two signature quilts (see page

152), one for adults and one for children, with people making a donation to sign their name on the quilt. Wendy Holland designed the quilts, using the emus, kangaroos and stars featuring in the logo for Quilt Australia. The adult's quilt has stars and strips sewn into rectangles, the children's quilt comprises strips arranged in hexagons, and is put together with triangles featuring kangaroos and emus.

Wendy silkscreen-printed the animals and people donated solid fabrics for signatures. Initially the strips were cut to size and the seam allowance marked in. During the first exhibition when the strips were available for signing, the folly of this became apparent. Children, particularly, found it difficult to keep their name within the lines, so when the strips were stitched together on the machine, parts of some signatures disappeared into the seams. After that the blocks were sewn together and the strips were signed on the block.

Black, felt-tipped laundry markers were used, and the signatures were then heat-set with a hot iron. The fabric had to be held tightly while being signed, and the writer cautioned not to hesitate with the pen on the fabric or a large ink blob would develop.

Pieced by Andrea and Annette Moylan, and quilted by Guild members, the quilts were enormously successful, not only in raising money, but for the enthusiasm they generated. Children and fond grandmothers, in particular, loved recording names and, when they came back the next year, were able to locate their names on the finished quilt. It remains as a record of the hard work involved in fund-raising, and of the contributions of many to an outstanding exhibition.

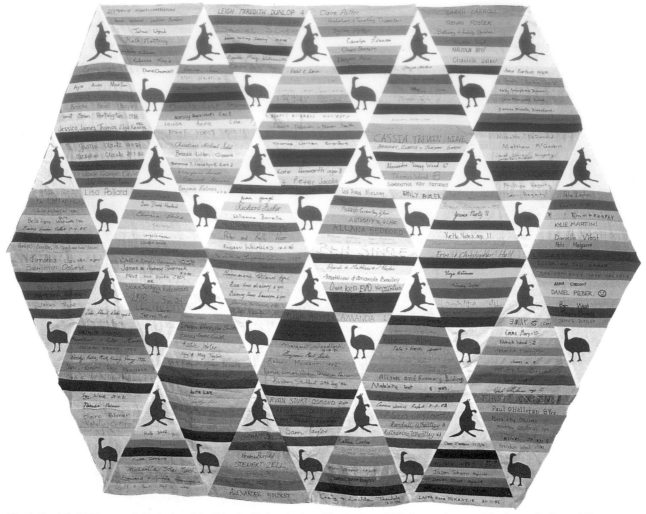

The Quilters' Guild Signature Quilt designed by Wendy Holland, pieced by Andrea O'Halloran, Annette Moylan and others. 130 cm x 250 cm (across centre), 200 cm (across top and bottom) (51 in. x 98½ in., 78½ in.). In the collection of The Quilters' Guild

CHILDREN'S QUILT

An account by June Cansdell who oversaw the design and execution of a quilt made by preschoolers:

I had seen in magazines quilts sewn by children, but always by much older children than those I had in mind. This quilt was to be my gift to the preschool on retirement after 15 years as a teaching assistant. The spontaneity in the drawings was achieved by involving the children in a conspiracy of secrecy: the director was away for the day, so we made the blocks then.

Drawings were made on squares of fabric that I had framed in cardboard. The fabric was 2.5 cm (1 in.) bigger on all sides than the cardboard window, which was held in position by masking tape. This made it easy to keep their work within the boundary, so none of it was lost in the seam allowances. I took four children at a time into the kitchen to paint the fabric.

I painted the hands of the three-year-olds so that they could record their handprints on fabric pieces. The four- and five-year-olds each painted a picture.

I had planned to arrange the blocks in a Patience Corner pattern, so that each block of

painted fabric was edged with strips on two sides. Decorative sketches showing aspects of preschool days and the children's names were added to the children's blocks. I then sewed the blocks together and handquilted around each handprint and each picture, quilting some of the elements.

The lively quilt thrilled the children, the director, and all who saw it. It now has pride of place at the preschool, hanging on a wall where it can be admired by all, but kept out of reach of small hands and strong sunlight.

St John's Preschool Class of 1987 by June Cansdell and students. 158 cm x 110 cm (62 in. x 43 ½ in.). Hand printed and painted. Machine pieced. Hand quilted

GREENWICH HOSPITAL QUILTS

An account by Dianne Finnegan, Past President of The Quilters' Guild:

Quilts are irrevocably associated with care and nurturing, and each year members of The Quilters' Guild make quilts for a community project. Hundreds of quilts have been made over the years for an adolescent unit, a home for the elderly, for deaf children, families staying at Ronald McDonald House (a place where the parents of sick children can stay) among others.

In 1988 when I was president of the Guild, quilts were being made for the palliative care ward at Greenwich Hospital, NSW. On my retirement from the position, I took on the job of Community Project Coordinator to complete the project. Guild members were asked to send in blocks measuring 30 cm (12 in.) plus seam allowance. The blocks were sorted into colours and sizes. It is amazing how much variation there can be in size from one 30 cm (12 in.) block to another! When they were sashed together creative sewing hid many imperfections. If a block was just too small, a narrow border was added so that it could be used.

Some groups would submit finished quilts that were coordinated blocks, but most of the blocks were different and were sewn into samplers. Towards the end, when the deadline was approaching, Yvonne Line organised a few women to mass-produce a number of simple Log Cabin quilts. One person cut strips, two worked on machines, one ironed and Yvonne oversaw operations. We speedily made six

quilts, some of which were tied and some machine quilted.

To sew all the quilts together and baste them for quilting, we were offered the use of the rehabilitation ward at the hospital, which is a very large, bright, airy room with solid tables and lots of floor space. Recovering patients were fascinated by the activity, and some of the old women offered their help, reminiscing while they stitched about things they had once made.

Smooth organisation ensured that the quilting bees were productive. A box of essentials was always on hand in case someone had forgotten something, and fabrics for sashing, borders and backing were washed and ready. Individuals or groups would volunteer to take basted quilts home to be quilted. The hospital provided morning and afternoon tea, and the busy women who gathered there enjoyed the company as much as the work.

It was wonderful to see the transformation of the ward when the quilts were put on the beds. Not only did the patients feel that they had come to a caring home rather than to an institution, but the staff appreciated the thought that had gone into the quilts and the colour that they had brought to the hospital environment. The quilts still provide a ready source of comment for visitors and are enjoyed by everyone.

The quilts were sturdily sewn and are washed in a domestic washing machine rather than in the hospital laundry. A couple of extra quilts were made so that there would always be one on every bed, even if some were in the wash. Guild members have undertaken to repair any that suffer wear over time. So far only one has disappeared, but it was

recovered soon after. Obviously it was appreciated!

FRIENDSHIP QUILT

An account by Dianne Finnegan:

The Wollstonecraft Quilters were keen to make friendship quilts for each member of the group, so I started them off. For my blocks I nominated a size (30 cm or 12 in.), with Hole in the Barn Door as the pattern, to be made up in shades of pink and grey. I provided templates and a stack of fabric from which the quilters could choose if they did not have the colours in their own stock. Each woman embroidered her name on the two blocks she made.

The blocks were a delight when they came back. Some people's interpretation of pink and grey came as a surprise: I would have called them green or blue. When I started putting the blocks together I realised that it was these blocks that gave the quilt a lift. It would have been boring without them.

I abutted the blocks with no sashing so that the different arrangements of light, medium and dark colours were highlighted. By varying them, a very simple pattern became much more complex. I had a beautiful piece of border fabric that I used, carefully mitring the corners so that the curve in the printed fabric flowed around them.

The quilt is a reminder of friendships and quilting days together.

Hole in the Barn Door. Hand and machine pieced by the Wollstonecraft Quilters. Assembled and machine quilted by Dianne Finnegan. 194 cm x 194 cm (76½ in. x 76½ in.). Nine patch

THE COAT OF ARMS

An account by Jennifer Lewis, member of The Australian Quilters' Association:

I felt the Australian Quilters' Association should do something as a group for Australia's Bicentenary, and Elva Hine

suggested something based on the Australian Coat of Arms. I was sent a publication by the Department of the Special Minister of State which gave a detailed description of the Coat of Arms, as well as information about its history and significance. This was invaluable for designing the shield, ensuring that the lions walked the right way, that the

stars had the right number of points, and that we used the correct terms. A larger print and a letter from the Prime Minister were enclosed.

Megan Terry, Elva Hine and I decided to divide the background into 22.5 cm (9 in.) squares for easier handling. I photographed the print and when we had finalised the size I projected the

Coat of Arms by members of the Australian Quilters' Association. 183 cm x 123 cm (72 in. x 48½ in.). Hand pieced, appliquéd and quilted

transparency on graph paper so that we could trace the outlines of branches, the kangaroo, the emu, and so on.

We bought two shades of gold material for the wattle, and one of blue and one of green for the leaves. The branches are made from an old continental quilt cover that had belonged to my son. It was in different brown shades and was nice and soft after much use and washing. The Southern Cross is made of white taratulle left over from a member's nursing days. The back of the quilt features The Royal Historical Society Bicentennial

Toile produced by Ascraft.

I organised the wattle makers, while Elva was to make the bow and Megan the shield. Heather Heathcote offered to make the star which she did beautifully, but when it was assembled we discovered the torse (the gold and blue wreath) was twisting the wrong way, so it had to be redone. Helen had already discovered the error but had hoped no one would notice!

Groups working on different aspects of the quilt chatted about anything but stitching, and the conversation ranged, whilst eating Mardi's sandwiches, from

the idiosyncracies of men, to genealogy, and peppermint leaves in cake tins. Mardi is a good source of information about imperial crowns. To keep the faith, she put a tiny cross in the crown on the quilt.

The difference in the gold circles representing the wattle, even though they were made from the same pattern, was incredible but has added charm to the finished quilt. I painted the kangaroo and for the first time ever I threw away the excess fabric only to realise that I needed some for a paw above the shield. One of Megan's reverse appliqué points around the shield edge became hidden under the paw, much to her disgust! Jenni Albanis did a lot of the embroidery and, with her beautiful work, made the emu's feathers a feature.

To hear the comments at the exhibition, particularly from overseas people, made the whole project worthwhile and we still have the quilt for future occasions.

THE WILLOUGHBY BANNERS

Textile artist Yvonne Line describes the process of making 14 banners:

To commemorate Australia's Bicentenary in 1988, the Willoughby Municipal Council decided that 14 textile banners representing the history of the community should be made to hang as a permanent record in the Civic Centre. In December 1985 we started designing the banners; the first people began sewing in March 1986; they were finished in October 1987; and the banners were hung in February 1988. It was a funded Bicentennial project and altogether just under 1000 people worked on it.

Following a lot of research, the community had indicated that it wanted to see a pictorial representation of the history of Willoughby, NSW, so old photographs were collected along with pictures of buildings that still exist. Of course you would need 200 banners to depict what everyone wanted.

Malcolm King was the artist who drew the designs from the information collected. His brief was to design the banners to represent 14 chronological stages. He says, "[The work] was to

Willoughby Banners by design artist Malcolm King and textile artist Yvonne Line, plus community helpers. 360 cm x 90 cm (141½ in. x 35½ in.). Machine appliquéd with some hand appliqué. Hand pieced. Hand quilted

identify a collective voice, it was to be decorative, instantly recognisable and relevant as a symbol of celebration . . . Once the subject matter of each banner was finalised, we considered the message, meaning, and the mood of each, and then we looked at colour, texture, design, direction, movement, weight, lustre and tonality."

It is now quite amazing to compare the finished work with the colour codes in Malcolm's designs — they are so close. I might have had to change a tone but I never actually changed a particular colour completely, even though most of the fabric, including my own fabric collection which I cart from one project to another, was donated. We only had to buy some of the larger pieces because, naturally, people only donated leftovers. We also had to buy the wadding (batting) and the backing.

We did not find a lot of experienced sewers coming forward, so at first it was a teaching process. With few needlework skills among the workers I had to bring the task back to the basics of sewing, and machine appliqué was used extensively. However, it was only necessary to show things to the sewers once or twice before their confidence grew. To begin with I gave them simple tasks: first one seam and then another.

Each banner was cut into panels 86 cm (35 in.) by 365 cm (146 in.) All the sections were divided up and sewn together later. One person, for example, would do just the hands in a banner, although that was not a beginner's piece as it had curves.

To begin with I had one day of preparation, then one day of sewing with interested members of the community, but as a band of more experienced people grew, I was able to do preparation during the day while they were sewing. Occasionally I would give people time to talk about the designs but the final colour and design decisions were my responsibility. It was really quite funny because the sewers were working on bits and pieces which didn't seem to connect until I started to build it up. For example, I would cut up certain colours, but no comments would be made until I was putting them together, and then the sewers would say "Oh! it *does* look all right!" They were too well mannered to say what they really thought while I was cutting out the pieces!

Actually it is quite interesting to see the number of people who went on to use the skills they had learned on other projects at home. It was a good offshoot from the project.

The banners were designed to fit the 14 acoustic panels spaced along the side walls of the Town Hall. Once they had been put up they were lit professionally. At the opening the Council was so proud. It was a wonderful project for a council to become involved in — it brought together the local government, residents and private sponsors to create something for the people.

GLOSSARY

accent a touch of bright colour

analogous harmony adjacent colours on the colour wheel

appliqué the sewing of one fabric shape onto another fabric

background fabric fabric used throughout the quilt top which appears to be behind the design

backstitch in a line of stitching, sewing back over the last gap. Used to finish a thread, for strength, or effect.

Baltimore Bride Album Quilt appliqué quilt in reds, greens and yellow on a white or cream background. Each block is sewn and signed by a different person. The quilt is a friendship quilt — made for a friend.

baste stitching or pinning the top, batt and lining together to prevent shifting during quilting

batt a sheet of stuffing that interlines the quilt top and lining. Used for warmth and/or to enhance the quilting.

bias a diagonal line at 45° to the long grain of fabric.

binding the folded strip of fabric that encloses the raw edges of the quilt

block the patterned unit of patchwork

Broderie Perse the appliqué of printed motifs from one fabric onto another

cartoon the full-scale drawing of the design on a quilt

Cathedral Window a quilt constructed of individual units folded, then sewn together with fabric windows over the joins

Celtic Appliqué appliqué designs based on those found in mediaeval texts and crafts. Bias strips outline the shapes.

Clamshell fishscale shapes that can be appliquéd together or used as a quilting design

complementary colours colours opposite to one another on the colour wheel

cording two layers of fabric sewn together with parallel lines of quilting through which cord is threaded

Crazy Patch irregularly shaped fabrics sewn together. The seams may be embroidered.

cross grain the weft or thread that runs at right angles to the warp in a woven fabric

echo quilting several rows of outline quilting that are equally spaced from a shape

English Paper Method the technique of basting fabric over paper shapes for accuracy before sewing shapes together. Hexagons are the most common shape

filler pattern an all-over pattern of quilting worked over large areas of the quilt

frame a square or rectangular frame of wood or plastic used to keep the three layers of a quilt taut during quilting

friendship quilt blocks made and signed by friends, joined and quilted and given to a person, usually for a special reason

foundation fabric onto which other surface fabrics are sewn for stability, e.g. in Crazy Patch

grain the line of warp thread running straight down the fabric

grey scale a regular progression from white to black. Any colour can be arranged in this way.

grid a network of regularly spaced lines subdividing a block, one set at right angles to the other

Hawaiian Appliqué snowflake design cut from one folded fabric and appliquéd onto a background fabric

hue pure colour

lattice a grid of strips separating individual blocks. Each individual strip is called a sash

lining fabric backing a quilt

Log Cabin traditional block with an isolated central square around which "logs" or strips of fabric are sewn

medallion quilt with a central feature surrounded by borders. Can be pieced and/or appliquéd, or wholecloth

mitre the 45° midline between two fabrics that join at a 90° angle

monochromatic colour scheme shades and tints of only one colour

motif a distinctive feature on a printed fabric.

multilayer cutting layers of fabric stacked and cut as one

offset one row displaced by one step from the next row

patchwork pieced or appliquéd work

picot the centrepoint of fabric folded and cut in Hawaiian Appliqué

piecing shapes of fabric seamed together

plaid chequered or tartan fabric

Prairie Points small triangles folded from squares arranged along the edge of a quilt

Puff Quilt a form of gathered patchwork

quilt textile with top, batt and lining

quilting stitch a stitch that secures the top, batt and lining of a quilt

Reverse Appliqué a design cut into the material and sewn in a stack of fabrics

sashing see **lattice**

scrap quilt usually a repeat block quilt worked in many

fabrics not closely coordinated

seam ripper unpicker

selvedge the closely woven edge of the fabric; designed to prevent unravelling

seminole patterns derived from cutting and recombining long strips of fabric that are seamed by machine

set the arrangement and orientation of blocks and lattice in a quilt

shadow appliqué appliqué overlain by transparent fabric and secured by quilting stitches

signature quilt a quilt top signed by many; often made as a fund-raiser

solid fabric in one, plain colour

Stained Glass bias strips, representing lead, covering seams in a stained-glass design, with different-coloured fabrics representing the glass

Suffolk Puffs a form of gathered patchwork

strip piecing long strips of fabric

sewn together in rows

template a pattern piece of any shape in a patchwork design. Made in plastic or cardboard that will not lose its shape

tessellation regular, interlocking shapes that cover an entire area

trapunto stuffed quilted areas

tying instead of holding the top, batt and lining together with lines of quilting, the quilt is tied by knots spaced across it

value tone, lightness or darkness of a colour

wagga Australian quilt originating in the Depression. Made from any available fabric and stuffed with old woollens, blankets or anything that would provide warmth

warp thread that runs lengthwise in woven fabric

whipstitch stitch that oversews two edges

wholecloth quilt with top made of only one piece of fabric to emphasise the quilting

SOME TRADITIONAL PATTERNS

Four Patch

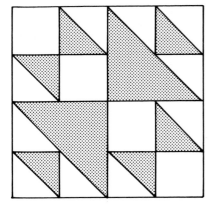

Crosses and Losses

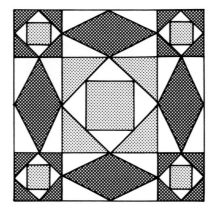

Storm at Sea

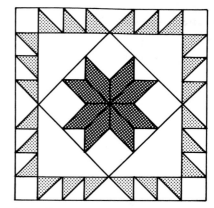

Star of Lemoyne

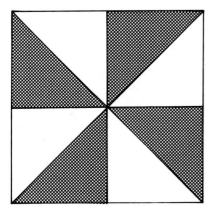

Windmill

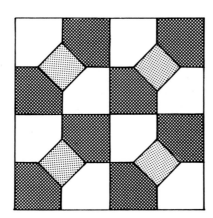

Bowtie

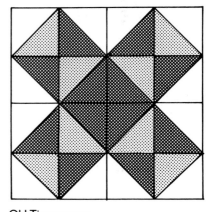

Old Tippencanoe

Five Patch

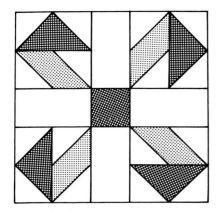

Jack in the Box

Wild Goose Chase

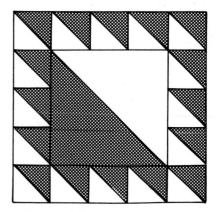

Lady of the Lake

Seven Patch

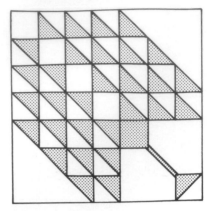

Pinetree

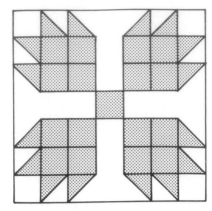

Bear's Paw

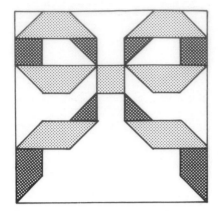

Bow

Nine Patch

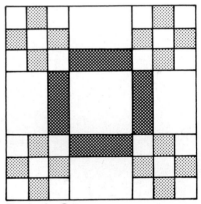

Puss in the Corner

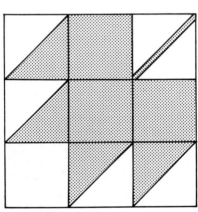

Maple Leaf

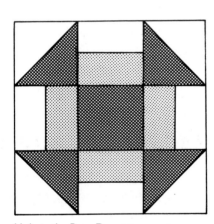

Hole in the Barn Door

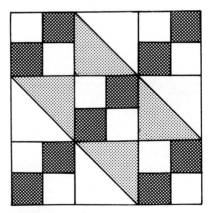

Jacob's Ladder

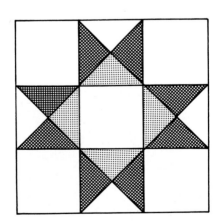

Ohio Star

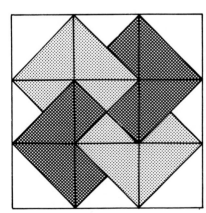

Card Trick

Curved Seams

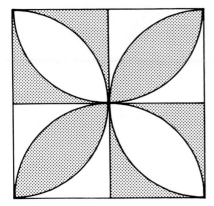

Orange Peel

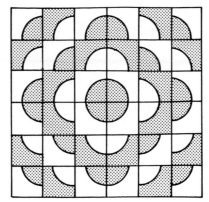

Drunkard's Path Arrangements

Eight-Point Star

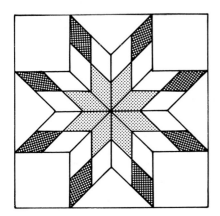

Virginia Star

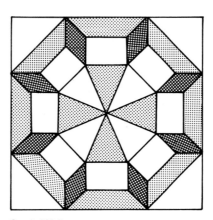

Castle Wall

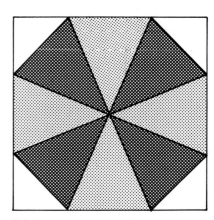

Kaleidoscope

Hexagon Arrangements

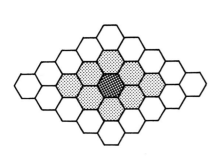

Hexagon Diamond

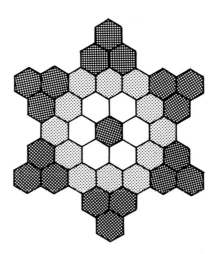

Hexagon Star

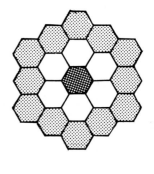

Grandmother's Flower Garden

Appliqué

Tulip

Butterfly

Wreath of Roses

Lady with Parasol

EMBROIDERY STITCHES

Embroidery stitches arranged by
June Scott Stevenson. Reproduced from *Embroidery Stitches*,
published by Ure Smith Pty Ltd, Sydney, 1942

CHAIN STITCH

FEATHER STITCH

LADDER CHAIN STITCH

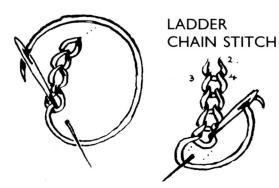

CHAIN FEATHER STITCH

MAGIC CHAIN STITCH

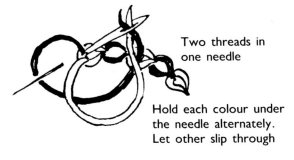

Two threads in one needle

Hold each colour under the needle alternately. Let other slip through

DOUBLE FISHBONE STITCH AND FRENCH KNOT

CABLE CHAIN STITCH

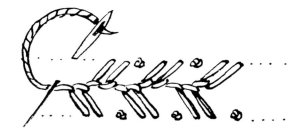

LEAVES

Fern
FEATHER STITCH

Group of Leaves
LAZY DAISY STITCH

BUTTONHOLE
FRENCH KNOT CHAIN

COUCHING
FRENCH KNOT
BUTTONHOLE

COUCHED OUTLINE

BACKSTITCH

LATTICE FILLING

OUTLINE STITCH
FRENCH KNOTS

Spray
FRENCH KNOTS

FLOWERS

Forget-Me-Nots

CROSS STITCH
CENTRE SMALL CROSS STITCH

Rose
BUTTONHOLE STITCH
FRENCH KNOTS CENTRE

HERRINGBONE STITCH

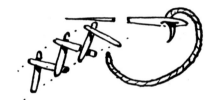

Daisy

LARGE WHITE, WOOL
CROSS STITCHES.
CENTRE SMALL ONES

May Blossom

SINGLE STITCH
THICK THREAD
FRENCH KNOT CENTRE

INTERLACED HERRINGBONE STITCH

Zinnia
SPACED BUTTONHOLE
CENTRE FINE

Delphiniums
SATIN STITCH

CHEVRON STITCH

Fuchsia

FRENCH
KNOT

LAZY DAISY
BUTTONHOLE COUCHING

Wattle
FINE BUTTONHOLE
OR EYELET STITCH

BIBLIOGRAPHY

QUILTMAKING IN AUSTRALIA

The Needlewoman (1927), quoted in Rae, J., *The Quilts of the British Isles*, Dutton, New York, 1987.

Isaacs, J., *The Gentle Arts: 200 Years of Australian Women's Domestic and Decorative Arts*, Lansdowne Press, NSW, 1987.

The Quilters' Guild, *Quilt Australia*, Bay Books, Sydney, 1988.

The Quilters' Guild, *Australian Quilts: The People and Their Art*, Simon & Schuster, Sydney, 1989.

Rolfe, M., *Patchwork Quilts in Australia*, Greenhouse, Victoria, 1987.

DESIGN

Itten, J., *The Elements of Color*, Van Nostrand Reinhold, New York, 1970.

Itten, J., *Design and Form*, Van Nostrand Reinhold, New York, 1975.

Lauer, D., *Design Basics*, Holt, Rinehart & Winston, New York, 1985.

Messent, J., *Embroidery and Nature*, Batsford, London, 1983.

Proctor, R. & Lew, J., *Surface Design for Fabric*, University of Washington Press, USA, 1984.

Richardson McKelvey, S., *Color for Quilters*, Yours Truly, Atlanta, 1984.

Wong, W., *Principles of Two Dimensional Design*, Van Nostrand Reinhold, New York, 1972.

PIECING

Beyer, J., *Patchwork Patterns*, EPM Publications, Virginia, 1979.

Beyer, J., *The Quilter's Album of Blocks and Borders*, EPM Publications, Virginia, 1980.

Bradkin, C., *The Seminole Patchwork Book*, Yours Truly, Atlanta, 1980.

Colby, A., *Patchwork*, Batsford, London, 1982.

Denton, S. & Macey, B., *Quiltmaking*, Nelson, Melbourne, 1987.

Hassel, C., *You Can Be a Super Quilter: A Teach Yourself Manual for Beginners*, Wallace-Homestead, Iowa, 1980.

Super Quilter II: Challenging Projects for the Advanced Quilters, Wallace-Homestead, Iowa, 1982.

Holstein, J., *The Pieced Quilt: An American Design Tradition*, New York Graphic Society, Boston, 1979.

James, M., *The Quiltmaker's Handbook*, Prentice Hall, New Jersey, 1978.

James, M., *The Second Quiltmaker's Handbook*, Prentice Hall, New Jersey, 1981.

Rolfe, M., *Australian Patchwork: A Step-by-Step Guide to Piecing, Quilting and Appliqué*. Curry O'Neil.

APPLIQUE

Avery, V., *The Big Book of Appliqué for Quilts and Banners, Clothes, Hangings, Gifts and More*, Charles Scribner's Sons, New York, 1978.

Bond, D., *Crazy Quilt Stitches*, Dorothy Bond, Oregon, 1981.

Brown, P., *The Book of Kells*, Thames and Hudson, Netherlands, 1980.

Horton, R., *Stained Glass Quilting Techniques*, (self published), Berkeley, 1978.

Scott Stevenson, J., *Embroidery Stitches*, Ure Smith, Sydney, n.d.

Sibbett, J., *Victorian Stained Glass Pattern Book*, Dover, New York, 1979.

Wiechec, P., *Celtic Quilt Designs*, Celtic Designs Co., Saratoga, 1980.

FABRIC MANIPULATION

Ericson, E., *Texture . . . A Closer Look*, Eric's Press, Hong Kong, 1987.

QUILTING

Colby, A., *Quilting*, Batsford, London, 1978.

Fanning, R. & T., *The Complete Book of Machine Quilting*, Chiltern Book Co., Pennsylvania, 1980.

Gillon, E., *Victorian Stencils for Design and Decoration*, Dover, New York, 1968.

Hornung, C., *Allover Patterns for Designers and Craftsmen*, Dover, New York, 1975.

Morgan, M. & Mosteller, D., *Trapunto and Other Forms of Raised Quilting*, Charles Scribner's Sons, USA, 1977.

Short, E., *Quilting Technique, Design and Application*, Batsford, London, 1974.

Svënnas, E., *Advanced Quilting*, Charles Scribner's Sons, New York, 1980.

PHOTOGRAPHIC CREDITS

All photography by Geordie McCrae except for the following:

Lee Atchinson 83
Douglas Baglin 150
Joanne Cowie 157
Roger Dekker 39
Diane Dowe 55
Craig Eades 137
Andrew Elton 8, 58, 124, 148
Terry Finnegan 14, 100, 145, 152
Dianne Firth 22
Victor France cover, 13, 16, 44, 45, 46, 103, 130

Fiona Gabens 27 (top left), 29
Irvine Green 18, 33, 38 (right), 80, 94 (top left and top right) 139, 156
Helen Gritscher 119
Helmut Gritscher 36
Craig Lamotte 15
Stuart Hay 30, 36 (right), 92, 97, 136
Barbara Macey 32
Tracey Nicholls 105
Andrew Payne 20
Moshe Rosenzveig 26, 36, 37, 49, 51, 92 (top), 114, 126, 133

Michael Saclier 109
Greg Somerville 24, 25 (bottom), 75
Robert Tawton 28, 83 (bottom), 92 (bottom)
Megan Terry 23, 110
Nancy Tingey 25 (top left and top right)
Ian Tudor 26, 38 (left), 50, 83, 146
Pierre van der Veer 10

INDEX OF QUILTMAKERS

INDEX